Authority And The Light Within

Edward Grubb

In the interest of creating a more extensive selection of rare historical book reprints, we have chosen to reproduce this title even though it may possibly have occasional imperfections such as missing and blurred pages, missing text, poor pictures, markings, dark backgrounds and other reproduction issues beyond our control. Because this work is culturally important, we have made it available as a part of our commitment to protecting, preserving and promoting the world's literature. Thank you for your understanding.

AUTHORITY AND THE LIGHT WITHIN

BY

EDWARD GRUBB, M.A.

AUTHOR OF "SOCIAL ASPECTS OF THE QUAKER FAITH."

THE JOHN C. WINSTON COMPANY
PHILADELPHIA
1908

AUTHORITY AND THE LIGHT WITHIN

PREFACE

THE purpose of this little book is to offer a contribution, however humble, towards the solution of the pressing problem of Authority in Religion. Is the final test of Truth to be found in a Church, or in a Book, or in human Reason, or in a spiritual Intuition? The Mystics, speaking generally, have adopted the fourth alternative: finding their court of final appeal in the Witness of God in the heart—which means, in effect, the Intuition of a spiritually-minded person. Among the Mystics a noteworthy place has been held by the Quakers, who have made the "Light Within," or the "Inward Light," the basis of their system of thought and practice.

There ought to be, as the outcome of the experience of the Society of Friends, a message for a world in doubt: for a world where systems of Authority have been overthrown by the advance of knowledge, and where many souls are helplessly drifting,—unable either to accept the outward authorities that are offered them, or to commit themselves with confidence to an Authority within.

Preface

Unfortunately, the Society of Friends, for reasons which are hinted at in the following pages, has produced very few thinkers. Its central thesis, of the paramount place of the Light Within, was expounded by Penn and Penington and Barclay in the terms of their own day; but the doctrine was never adequately harmonised, either with a sound conception of Authority, or with the Divine revelation which they, in common with more orthodox Christians, found in the Christ of history. Out of this inconsistency has come division within the Society of Friends itself, and to it we may probably look for one of the chief though hidden causes of its failure to move the world.

In the belief of the writer, the Society of Friends is in possession of a truth that the world needs; but, if this truth is to be proclaimed effectively, it must be set free, not alone from its antiquated expression, but from serious inconsistencies of thought. It needs to be restated in modern language, and in the light of modern knowledge.

The message of the early Quakers was at once mystical and evangelical; and, in the writer's view, it is possible so to restate that message as to conserve at once the catholicity of the mystic's appeal to

Preface

universal Light, the sobriety of the faithful student of religious history, and the fervour of evangelical belief in Christ.

Some steps towards such a restatement have already been taken by Dr. Rufus M. Jones, of Haverford College, Pennsylvania, in his "Social Law in the Spiritual World" and other works. To him the writer is much indebted, not alone for luminous and helpful thoughts, but also for friendly counsel and encouragement.

EDWARD GRUBB.

3, GEORGE STREET,
 CROYDON,
  February, 1908.

CONTENTS

CHAPTER		PAGE
I.	THE NATURE OF AUTHORITY	11
II.	THE AUTHORITY OF THE CHURCH	18
III.	THE AUTHORITY OF THE BIBLE	27
IV.	THE AUTHORITY OF THE BIBLE (*continued*)	35
V.	THE AUTHORITY OF CHRIST	45
VI.	THE AUTHORITY OF THE SPIRIT	55
VII.	WHAT IS THE LIGHT WITHIN?	63
VIII.	THE QUAKERS ON THE LIGHT WITHIN	70
IX.	THE WEAKNESS OF QUAKERISM	78
X.	THE LIGHT WITHIN AND REASON	88
XI.	THE LIGHT WITHIN AND REASON (*continued*)	96
XII.	THE LIGHT WITHIN AND CONSCIENCE	104
XIII.	THE LIGHT WITHIN AND ATONEMENT	112
XIV.	THE LIGHT WITHIN AND THE HOLY SPIRIT	120
XV.	SUMMARY	127
XVI.	CONCLUSION	135

AUTHORITY AND THE LIGHT WITHIN

I

THE NATURE OF AUTHORITY

The old cry "What is Truth?" still echoes the questioning of many hearts, and we long for an authoritative answer. The craving is strong within us for infallible guidance; for someone, whom we can implicitly trust, to tell us with certainty what we ought to believe, how we ought to act. In our ignorance and weakness, it seems vain to hope that we, by our own efforts, can attain to truth of knowledge or truth of conduct. "O God, my boat is so small, and Thy ocean is so vast!"

Control of the individual, of his thoughts and his activities, by a knowledge larger than his own, is what we call Authority. It is obviously a principle that covers a great part of the individual's life. Each one of us is in presence of a larger human whole, in dependence on which we are, to a very large extent, compelled to think and act.

From our earliest years we are placed under Authority; our lives are regulated by parents and teachers; the truths they hold we are taught to

Authority and the Light Within

believe. Even in adult life we are surrounded by authority at every turn; the laws of the State and the municipality direct our actions at home, in the streets, in business, in ways of which we normally are but little conscious. And, even in the country that is most free, where thought is untrammelled by State or Church, our beliefs are in large part moulded by others. Few of us have ever had the opportunity of forming really independent conclusions, even on the theories that underlie the commonest concerns of life. For the most part we accept from others belief in the earth's rotation, in the chemical constitution of the air we breathe and the food we eat, in the outlines of the history of our country, without ourselves having put these things to the test. All of us who are not original investigators, and many who are, in hundreds of matters, every day we live, accept the statements of those in whose ability and honesty we have confidence. *Every one who can see further than others into the truth of things speaks with some authority*, and that authority is recognised.

Thus the individual is never an isolated unit; he grows up and maintains his life in relation to, and largely in dependence on, the Society in which he finds himself; he is, all through his life, compassed round with Authority. We do not start life with no capital; we enter upon the accumulated inheritance of the ages. We have, of course, the power to set Authority at defiance; children disobey, men break the law, new theories are started in opposition to those commonly accepted. And it is impossible to

The Nature of Authority

apply to such acts of defiance universal censure or universal praise. They may be due merely to the lawless self-assertion of the individual; on the other hand, they may be the very condition of human progress. "We must obey God rather than men," said the Apostles; and it is largely by such refusal to obey that the liberties have been won which we now enjoy. At the foundation of all our science lies the revolt against Authority led by Copernicus, Bacon, Galileo; our spiritual freedom flows from the "heresies" of Wycliffe, Luther, Fox.

By the light of burning heretics Christ's bleeding feet I track,
Toiling up new Calvaries ever with the cross that turns not back;
And these mounts of anguish number how each generation learned
One new word of that grand *Credo* which in prophet hearts hath burned,
Since the first man stood God-conquered, with his face to heaven upturned.

It follows, then, that the Authority which human Society has over the individual is not final or absolute, but is limited and relative. The attempt to make it more than this is self-destructive. For Society is composed of individuals; and it is only as the individual expands, develops, grows strong, that Society itself prospers. To crush the individual, as he was crushed under the mediæval Church, and as, many of us think, he would be crushed under some modern "collectivist" Utopias, would be to destroy the very material out of which a vigorous society can be constructed.

Over against Authority stands the Autonomy of the individual; and the true function of Authority is to bring that autonomy to the front, and thus gradually

Authority and the Light Within

efface itself. The true parent strives to train his children to obey the right from choice, not from compulsion; the true teacher draws on his pupils to form their own opinions from independent examination of the facts. That State is the healthiest in which the law is least often put in motion, in which individuals have been so taught and trained that they do of themselves such things as the law directs. "Like every good teacher," says Auguste Sabatier, "Authority should labour to render itself useless."[1]

Goodness which is such under compulsion is only half goodness; truth which is embraced at second hand is only half truth. The only real goodness is that which is the free choice of the individual; the only effectual truth is that which he discerns for himself to be grounded in fact and reason. Authority, therefore, must always seek to be transformed into autonomy. It "can maintain itself only by becoming more moral, by placing its supporting point always less apart from man, always more essentially within the man himself."[2] This autonomy of the individual is something wholly different from mere self-assertion; it is nothing else than inward consecration to truth and goodness; and, so far therefore from leading to anarchy, it brings with it the highest harmony.

So far we have been dealing with Authority mainly as it concerns matters of ordinary life and knowledge; we have now to consider whether the case is different

---

[1] "Religions of Authority and the Religion of the Spirit," p. xxvii.
[2] A. Sabatier, *op. cit.*, p. xxxii.

The Nature of Authority

in those concerns of highest moment which we call distinctively spiritual or religious. It is here, no doubt, in this region where experience passes "behind the veil" of time and sense, and where in consequence the way seems dim to those whose spiritual senses are not acute, that the cry for authoritative guidance is most often and most loudly heard. There are many who will admit to the full what has been said about the limited and provisional character of authority in common life, who yet in the religious sphere demand something more final and conclusive. Is there, then, such an authority? All will allow that, if any knowledge is possible of God and of His will, the ultimate source of such knowledge, the ultimate authority, can be nowhere else than in God Himself; and that that authority is final, absolute, and infallible.

But how is that Divine authority mediated to men? The knowledge of God is wholly different in kind from our knowledge of facts; God is not one phenomenon among other phenomena; He never was nor will be perceptible by men's outward senses. "God is Spirit"; "no man hath seen God at any time." The voice of God is heard by us individually and in secret; unless in some way it could take outward form, it could not be applied, in the simple way that facts can, to afford a common test of truth.[1] Hence men have felt the need of some outward institution to embody the Divine authority, in order to

---

[1] This is where some of the Quakers went wrong when they spoke of the Spirit as a "rule" of faith and practice.

Authority and the Light Within

make it available, something that shall speak as with His voice, directing and controlling men's thoughts and lives. It is this want of the human spirit that Roman Catholics have sought to supply with an infallible Church, and Protestants with an infallible Bible.

In subsequent chapters I hope to examine how far these supposed infallible outward authorities have made good their claim. Meanwhile, assuming that an inward knowledge of God is possible for men, though knowledge with the outward senses is not, it may be noted that there is a large field, even in the spiritual sphere, in which that limited and relative authority of which I have already spoken may be exercised. That which anyone can discern of God, in his own religious experience, gives him so far a measure of authority; those who "see" further than others, the prophets and apostles of humanity, have more authority. He who came from God, and lived ever near to the Father's heart (John i. 18), had it without measure. That which God has made known to men concerning Himself, however imperfectly understood, has been recorded in literature and embodied in institutions; the religious experience of those who have gone before us is there enshrined; and each one of us, who seeks God for himself, will naturally therefore "put himself to school within a larger experience than his own." He will not presumptuously expect that he can be saved the trouble of the search for God, either by having truth infallibly dealt out to him from Church or Bible, or by having it miraculously revealed to him

The Nature of Authority

de novo. He will make humble use of the authorities around him, remembering that they are not absolute and final; that their function is to train him in original powers of spiritual perception; that Authority does its true work by being transformed into Autonomy; that the light without him is intended to develop the Light Within.

II

THE AUTHORITY OF THE CHURCH

IN the last chapter it was pointed out that the craving for an infallible outward authority in religion arises from the nature of spiritual or religious truth. The deepest truth, the centre of our life, the basis of all reality, is not to be discovered by the outward senses. God is deeper than all phenomena, and He cannot, like matters of ordinary knowledge, be subjected to sensuous demonstration. We cannot appeal to facts, and say "Lo here!" or "Lo there!" We walk by faith, not by sight; eye hath not seen, nor ear heard, the things of the Spirit. God manifests Himself to the inner consciousness; His witness is within.

Hence it is that men have tried to find and establish an outward authority, by which the declarations of the inward witness may be tested: some divine institution, some external rule of faith and life, which may be used as an infallible criterion to mark off truth from falsehood, right from wrong. Chief among these supposed infallible authorities is that of the Catholic Church.

The thought of an infallible Church is not that in which most of us have been trained, and some may find it difficult to understand. And yet to a Catholic it appears simple and satisfying. The Church is

The Authority of the Church

thought to be a visible and permanent corporation, instituted by Jesus Christ, and charged by God Himself with the function of saving men, and teaching them what they ought to believe and do. God Himself is in it, just as He was in Jesus Christ. The Church, indeed, carries on the Incarnation, which is thus brought close to us, and is no longer an event of the past alone. There are two elements in the Church, divine and human, the former being the soul that vivifies the latter, which without it would be wholly dead. Hence outside the Church there is no salvation, no saving knowledge of the truth. God being thus incarnated in the Church, she is by her very nature infallible; otherwise God Himself would be guilty of error or deception.

But of whom does the Church consist? There are two definitions, a larger and a smaller: the first including all who profess its faith and share its sacraments; the latter comprising only the sacerdotal order to which the supernatural powers of Jesus Christ and His Apostles have been handed on. "To the latter pertains the office of governing and teaching; to the former that of obeying and receiving instruction."[1] It should be noted that the definition has nothing to do with inward and personal experiences like repentance and conversion; for a visible Church must be defined by outward marks that are manifest to all. The Church, in the Catholic idea, may have rebellious

---

[1] A. Sabatier, "Religions of Authority," p. 89. This is why churches are built with a "choir" separated from the rest of the church by a railing and steps. The "choir" is the priests' church, the rest that of the worshippers.

Authority and the Light Within

subjects, just as a State may; but a baptized person, however sinful or unbelieving, is and remains a child of the Church until cut off by formal excommunication.

Authority, it will be seen, resides not in the Church in the larger sense, but in the hierarchy: it comes to the Bishops as a supernatural gift by the laying on of hands in unbroken line from the Apostles themselves, and through them in measure to the clergy as a whole. But how is it exercised, and who pronounces the final verdict in the case where lesser authorities disagree? Three answers have been given to this question: first, that it is the General Council of the Bishops; second, that it is the Pope; and third, that it is in the agreement of these two, the Pope and the Council. At the present day, however, only one of these answers has any living interest. For in 1870 the Council signed its own death-warrant by pronouncing the dogma of the Pope's Infallibility.

Fantastic as it seems to Protestants, this may well be regarded as the logical outcome of the Catholic theory. Without attempting the task of proving this in detail, we may notice one consideration: that, if the Pope is not infallible, the Church is not infallible either; for then the Church, through her Council, has made a mistake in declaring him to be so. In fact, the dogma has destroyed the power that created it, and annihilated its own foundations; it has made the whole idea of Church authority one great *petitio principii*. "I believe in the infallible Pope, because the Pope has pronounced himself infallible."

The Authority of the Church

The truth is that, when the idea of the Church's infallible authority is looked at in the light of history and reason, it is discovered to be entirely without foundation. There is nothing, in the recorded teaching of Jesus or His Apostles, that in the remotest degree foreshadows it—except the words said (in Matt. xvi. 18, 19) to have been addressed to Peter. These words are not alluded to by any writer before nearly the close of the second century; and, even in the third century, the interpretation which found in them a basis for the paramount authority of the Roman Bishop, as the successor of Peter, was strongly opposed by Tertullian, Origen, and Cyprian.[1] They are under grave suspicion (being absent in Mark) of having been inserted through ecclesiastical influences.

There is no clear evidence that Peter was ever Bishop of Rome; indeed, the idea of an apostle-bishop is self-contradictory, since apostles were essentially itinerant and bishops resident. There was no single bishop at Rome before the reign of Hadrian, about 150 A.D., the varying lists of early bishops found in certain writings having been invented to prove a case. " In the reign of Trajan and the early years of Hadrian the Church of Rome was still living under presbyterial rule."[2] That is to say, at Rome, as in other churches, the presbyters, elders, or bishops, who were originally chosen by the congregation, gradually gained more and more authority, and their president finally became

[1] A. Sabatier, *op. cit.*, p. 119.
[2] See Acts xxviii., Epistles to Romans and Philippians, 1 Peter, etc. Also the Epistle of Clement of Rome, the "Shepherd" of Hermas, and the letter of Ignatius to the Romans. (A. Sabatier, *op. cit.*, p. 105.)

Authority and the Light Within

"the bishop" *par excellence*. The epistle of Clement shows the kind of conflict that often arose between the presbyters, who were servants of a special community, and the "apostles, prophets and teachers," who were for the most part in the service of the church at large. It was as the gifts of the latter declined, as the life of the Spirit grew feeble, as doubtful teaching and unhelpful "prophecy" came to the front, that the demand for order in the church developed the power of the bishop. "In proportion as Christianity grew inwardly cold, it felt the necessity of strengthening its external unity by a more closely-knit organisation."[1]

Church authority, therefore, as exercised through the bishops, indicates not the presence of the Spirit in the hierarchy, but its absence in the Church at large. It means the displacement by a human organisation of the free and spontaneous working of the Spirit which had characterised the early days; it marks the coming to the front of the human and not the divine element in the Church.[2]

And, accordingly, examination of the history reveals no such supernatural coherence and consistency, in the decisions of Councils and of Popes, as the theory of infallible authority would require. The paramount position of the Bishop of Rome was not recognised by the other bishops without fierce conflicts; by the Eastern Church it has never been recognised at all;

---

[1] A. Sabatier, *op. cit.*, p. 82.
[2] Montanism was in essence an attempt to throw off the yoke of the hierarchy, and revert to the earlier freedom of prophecy. Unfortunately, its worked-up fervours were not, for the most part, "in the life."

The Authority of the Church

but the same causes that pushed to the front the president of a local presbytery gradually transformed the church at large from a democracy to a monarchy. And the history of that monarchy is exactly similar to that of any other. The most worldly weapons for acquiring and maintaining power were not despised. The "False Decretals" of the pseudo-Isidore, a series of apocryphal decisions by mythical Popes, constituting "the most colossal and bare-faced fraud of which history has to tell," became the foundation of Roman canon law and of the universal theocracy aimed at by Gregory VII. and Innocent III. What sort of infallibility do we find in Vigilius (537—555), who wrote to some "monophysite" bishops saying that he had come to hold their view (that Christ had a single and not a double "nature"), but that they were to keep his opinion secret lest it should injure his candidature for the See of Rome (which he succeeded in gaining), and who afterwards more than once changed his view? Or in Honorius (625—638) who was pronounced heretical and accursed by the sixth Ecumenical Council and by his successors, for holding that in Jesus Christ there was only a single will?[1] This one example, though of little importance in itself, shows conclusively that the dogma of papal infallibility is a mere afterthought. It is a theory, developed later, to account for the power which the Pope had actually gained.

What are we to make of the Council of Constance, which cited two rival Popes to appear before it and

[1] See Martineau, "Seat of Authority in Religion," pp. 139—143.

Authority and the Light Within

deposed them, electing a third? Either it was acting with authority, or without. If with authority, it was superior to the papacy, and the Pope therefore not infallible; if without, Martin V. was no Pope and there is a breach in the succession: the cardinals he created were illegitimate, and all Popes since his time invalidly elected.

Where, again, do we find infallibility in the repeated decrees that insist on the reality of witchcraft, or in those that condemned the views of Copernicus and Galileo—decrees which the Church dares now neither to defend nor to withdraw? The truth is clear, that the Church of Rome has made the same sort of mistakes into which every other human institution is liable to fall, and that its infallibility can only be held by those who surrender themselves wholly to it, deliberately blinding their eyes to obvious facts of history.

If we turn for a moment to the more limited authority which is claimed for the Church by Anglicans, a measure of the same objection applies here also. The Anglican Church is essentially a compromise between Romanism and Protestantism, and nothing rigorous or severely logical can be looked for in it. While there is much that is true and beautiful in the ideal of the Church presented by men like Bishop Gore, it is spoiled by the notion of the apostolical succession—a dream as empty of historical reality as that of papal infallibility itself, and one which, by denying "validity" to Nonconformist sacraments, is the fruitful parent of religious strife and hatred.

The Authority of the Church

"Authentic history mentions no example of a bishop consecrated by an apostle, and to whom an apostle might have transmitted, by this institution, either the totality or a part of his powers. . . . An interval of more than half a century separates the disappearance of the apostles from the appearance of the first bishop in the Catholic sense."[1] Clement of Rome, writing early in the second century to encourage obedience to the "bishops" (or presbyters) at Corinth, does not invoke any apostolic authority, but turns to Moses and the prophets. The Pastoral Epistles, which probably date from the same period, know nothing of single bishops, but presuppose several at a time governing the same community.[2] The gift that is in Timothy has come to him by the laying on of hands —not only of the apostle, but of the presbytery (1 Tim. iv. 14 ; 2 Tim. i. 6).

And yet, beneath all the extravagances and unrealities that have marked the Catholic notion of authority, there is at least this solid nucleus of truth : that the Holy Spirit is a present possession of the Church, and that in the unity of the Christian consciousness there is an authority, not absolute and final, but real and living, which has its place in correcting the vagaries of individual illumination. The Spirit did not forsake the Church when the last page of the Bible was penned ; nor was it ever the monopoly of any priestly caste. In the primitive Church the gift

---

[1] A. Sabatier, *op. cit.*, p. 91.
[2] See Titus i. 5, 7, noting that the "elders" and the "bishop" refer to the same persons.

Authority and the Light Within

of the Spirit, and this alone, made a true Christian; and whatever authority was recognised as pertaining to the Church had its seat in the full assembly of believers. And that was surely the intention of its Founder.

III

THE AUTHORITY OF THE BIBLE

It has often been said that, while the Catholics find their ultimate authority in an infallible Church, the Protestants try to discover it in an infallible Bible. Historically speaking, this is broadly true; and, just in so far as Protestants actually depend upon an infallible external authority, their position does not differ in principle from that of Catholics. It is simply the substitution of one supposed infallibility for another. The Protestant who believes that Jonah was literally swallowed and cast out by a fish, simply because he finds such a statement in the Bible, is in exactly the same intellectual position as the Catholic who believes that Mary was born sinless (the dogma of the " Immaculate Conception "), not because he discerns it to be true, but because the Church tells him it was so.

Moreover, the logical and spiritual advantage, in the conflict between the two, rests unquestionably with the Catholic. For, to prove his position, the Protestant has to mark off a certain set of books (the "canon" of Scripture), the only guarantee for which comes through the tradition of the very Church whose authority he denies; and he is substituting, for an authority living and close at hand—able (so the Catholic believes) to guide in new conditions and answer new questions as they arise—an authority that

Authority and the Light Within

is of the past alone, fixed in a volume of ancient writings that can never be altered or adapted.

But, in point of fact, few Protestants have held, with rigorous logic, the position that is here attributed to them. Luther and the early Reformers were very far indeed from so stultifying themselves. They had found for themselves a new standing before God, by coming into a direct relation with Jesus Christ, entirely apart from obedience to the authority of the Church. Luther, it has been said, re-discovered the worth of the individual, and raised him erect upon his feet in the very presence of God. Hence the "autonomy of the individual," which (as we have seen) is the higher stage for which authority prepares the way, was a part of the very air they breathed. And so Luther constantly appealed to an inward witness, "the Testimony of the Spirit," deep in the heart of the individual, to guarantee the truth of Scripture itself. This was the position of Calvin also. Moreover, Luther was very far from accepting bodily the canon of Scripture as the Church of Rome handed it over. He criticised it with considerable sharpness, excluding from the list of truly inspired writings the Book of Esther, as too much filled with "heathen naughtiness," and calling the Epistle of James, since it did not seem to him to teach justification by faith in Christ, "a veritable epistle of straw." Calvin doubted the authenticity of the second Epistle of Peter, and, from similar doubts, never commented upon the Book of Revelation. The Reformed Confessions of faith, even when they give the

The Authority of the Bible

traditional list of books, are careful to explain that they are to be held and recognised as inspired by God, " not so much because of the unanimous consent of the Church, as in virtue of the inward witness and persuasion of the Holy Spirit, by whom we are made wise to discover and set apart these from other ecclesiastical books."[1]

Unfortunately, the exigencies of the great controversy with Rome were very pressing, and the early Reformers never allowed the seeds of free and unfettered criticism of the Biblical documents, which Luther dropped, to germinate and grow. The lapse of logic involved in the assumption that the inward witness of the Holy Spirit will necessarily guarantee the inspiration of precisely those books which the Church tradition has handed down, has been one of the inherent weaknesses of Protestantism. The Church of Rome, indeed, had a secondary list of books, which she also regarded as in some degree inspired, which were known as the Apocrypha. The Reformers never explained how it was that the Holy Spirit showed them that all in the first list were full of Divine authority, while all in the second list were not. It is not too much to say that no one's "inward witness" tells him that Ecclesiastes and Esther are fully inspired by God, while Ecclesiasticus and the Wisdom of Solomon are only human writings. Whoever holds this view does so because he fancies there is some other authority, outside his own spiritual insight, which guarantees the first list

[1] A. Sabatier, "Religions of Authority," p. 159.

Authority and the Light Within

and not the second. And, when closely examined, this "other authority" is found to reside in acts of Jewish synagogues and rabbis, to which, therefore, a direct divine inspiration is, actually, if unconsciously, attributed. In like manner, the only ground for assigning plenary divine authority to the second Epistle of Peter is that it was included in the sacred canon, in the fourth century, by a Council of the Catholic Church,—that Church whose authority in other matters the Protestant rejects.

Apart from the flaws in logic which have been pointed out, the idea that the Scriptures as we have them are the pure and unadulterated "Word of God," as many Protestants still try to believe, is frankly impossible. Without going into the facts revealed by recent Biblical criticism, the sheer incredibility of what is still regarded by many as Protestant orthodoxy may be seen from a few general considerations. Let us grant at once that God is infallible, and assume that it is His will to reveal His truth to men. The inference that the Bible contains nothing but that truth, pure and unalloyed, involves not only Divine infallibility, but four separate human infallibilities, all impossible.

(*a*) It assumes that God's truth was infallibly apprehended by prophets and apostles and other Biblical writers—unless, indeed, it prefers to regard them as mere unconscious automata.

(*b*) It assumes that the truth, whether consciously apprehended or not, was infallibly expressed in human language.

(*c*) It assumes that the words so written have been infallibly transmitted to us.

(*d*) It assumes that we can infallibly interpret those expressions.

The Authority of the Bible

Now, a very little thought must convince anyone that none of these infallibilities has, in fact, existed.

(*a*) The Biblical writers show the clearest evidences of a partial and not a complete enlightenment. This is positively taught by our Lord in the Sermon on the Mount (Matt. v. 21 and ff.). The author (or authors) of the later part of the Book of Isaiah—truly inspired, if anything in the Old Testament is so—attributed human evil and sin to Jehovah (Isaiah xlv. 7, lxiii. 17). Paul definitely expected that, in his own lifetime, Jesus would come again (1 Thess. iv. 15-17). On the assumption that the writers were automata, these mistakes would have to be assigned to God Himself.

(*b*) The idea that Divine truth could be infallibly expressed in human words, can only be held by those who have never properly considered what language is. Missionaries to the heathen often find that there is no native word to express what they want to say; and all human language is, in like manner, in some degree inadequate. All the words by which we try to express the deeper realities are metaphors, derived from our sensuous experiences: spirit is "breath," existence is what "stands out," substance what "stands under," and so forth. Hence any form of words, applied to spiritual things, can do no more than *suggest* a great deal that words can never fully cover. Words are nothing more than attempts to express ideas and experiences; how much they express depends upon the ideas and experiences of the society in which they pass current; and, as this develops, the meanings continually change. Hence, to speak

Authority and the Light Within

of any infallible revelation in human language is absurd.

(c) The least study of manuscripts, or even of the Revised Version, shows at once that the words of the Biblical writers have not been infallibly transmitted to us. The existing MSS. show many thousands of variations; and the original text is gone absolutely beyond recall. In the case of the Old Testament, there is evidence that, at a certain point in its history, the problem was simplified by the expedient of destroying all variants but one.

(d) Infallible interpretation is as impossible as infallible language. As we have seen, words can do no more than *suggest* much that can never be fully expressed by them; and what they suggest will depend in large measure on the experience of the reader. "God is love" means little or much to us, according to the poverty or richness of our experience of what love is. "The Devil," to a mediæval person, suggested a material being, black in colour, with horns and a tail. It does not suggest that to us. And, in very many cases, the meaning of Biblical passages is really doubtful. "Lovest thou me more than these?" may mean, grammatically, "more than thou lovest these," or "more than these love me." It is said that the number of possible interpretations of Gal. iii. 20, "Now a mediator is not a mediator of one, but God is one," is between 200 and 300. The science of Biblical exegesis is the endeavour to discover, with all the light that historical research can throw, what the Biblical writers actually meant to say, and to put

The Authority of the Bible

ourselves at their point of view that we may be able sympathetically to explain their meaning. This science, though a measure of agreement is happily being reached among competent students, is still very far from complete; and, so long as each person, without the necessary knowledge, tries to interpret at his own sweet will, we can see the necessity, which the Catholic is never weary of urging, for an infallible Church to interpret the Bible to us.

That is to say, if we insist on making the Bible an infallible outward authority, we cannot stop there, but must go on to the Catholic position of an infallible Church. Happily, there is no need to take up any such impossible and dangerous position. The need for an infallible authority in the early Church was only felt as its spiritual life began to wane; and, as we hope to show more fully in the next chapter, it was so in the Reformed Churches of the sixteenth century. So long as the glow of a new spiritual experience, in direct contact with the Spirit of Christ, was felt in the heart, its light shone upon the pages of Scripture, and simple souls found their needs were satisfied without any dogma of infallibility. The "testimony of the Spirit," the answer of the inward witness, was felt to be sufficient. Truth, Calvin said, makes itself directly recognised as such by its intrinsic character, as things black and white reveal their colour to the eyes, and things sweet and bitter reveal their flavour. "Only pious hearts know this," wrote Zwingli, "for faith does not depend upon the discussions of men, but has its seat, and rests

Authority and the Light Within

itself invincibly, in the soul. It is an *experience* which everyone may have. It is not a doctrine, a question of knowledge, for we see the most learned men who are ignorant of this thing which is the most salutary of all."

If only the Reformed Churches had followed up this leading, instead of squandering their souls in the barren wastes of intellectual sophistication, how much better might the world have been!

IV

THE AUTHORITY OF THE BIBLE—
(continued)

THE first Reformers, as we have seen, were far from making their Christian faith depend upon the infallible outward authority of the Bible as it had come down to them through Church tradition. The essence of their faith was the consciousness of a direct personal relation with God through Jesus Christ, and the glow of this personal relation shed light enough upon the pages of the Bible to enable the reader, so Luther believed, to separate the pure gold from the alloy he found there.

Nominally the Reformed Churches retained belief in the "inward witness" of the Holy Spirit as a guarantee for the truth of Scripture; but, as their inward fire died down, and their position had to be made good, on the one hand against the authority of the Roman Church, and on the other against the "illuminates" whose revolt against authority was tending towards anarchy and individual licence, their position became more and more an intellectual one, and their conception of authority purely external. They took the fatally easy path of identifying, as Luther had never done, the canonical Scriptures with the "Word of God" that was in them, and, while professing that the Holy Spirit assured them of their

Authority and the Light Within

infallible truth, devoted all their energies to the vain attempt to prove the position by argument. The result was a desert of sophistication in which the pure water of the revelation of God contained in the Bible was well-nigh swallowed up and lost. It is probably this, more than any other cause, that explains the Catholic reaction of the early seventeenth century, when, in several of the European countries, nearly everything was lost that Protestanism seemed to have gained.

It would be unprofitable to follow, with weary steps, the lines of argument by which the Protestant divines of the seventeenth and eighteenth centuries struggled to prove the impossible. A favourite method was to prove the Bible from the Bible, using texts like "All scripture is given by inspiration of God," as if they asserted the literal infallibility of the particular writings that have come down to us. The miracles were appealed to as guaranteeing the supernatural character of the revelation; but, if anyone asked for a guarantee of the miracles, the answer was simply, they are in the Bible. Thus the argument revolved in a vicious circle, comparable exactly to that by which the Pope's infallibility is supported by Catholics. "I believe in the infallibility of the Bible, because the Bible declares itself to be infallible."

It was in reference to such pastors as these divines, "blind mouths," that Milton wrote, in scorn, "The hungry sheep look up and are not fed." It was against such as these that protests were made by the mystics and "illuminates," who, alleging that a light

The Authority of the Bible

from God was in them, superior to any that could be borrowed at second-hand from the Scriptures, were known in England by the opprobrious name of "Ranters." It was against such ministry as that of these divines that George Fox and the early Quakers came forth, with the message of a present revelation from a living Christ, not prisoned in the pages of a book; from One who could speak, here and now, to the condition of individual hearts.

Quakerism was essentially a revival of spiritual religion, at a time when the Reformation had spent its force. It was the appeal from a dead to a living God—from one whose word was a fossil, stored carefully in a museum, to one who still spoke and breathed in the hearts of living men. The account Fox gives in his "Journal" (Vol. I., ch. iii.) of his interruption of the preacher at the parish church at Nottingham, in 1649, makes this very clear.

> When I came there, all the people looked like fallow ground, and the priest, like a great lump of earth, stood in his pulpit above. He took for his text these words of Peter, "We have also a more sure Word of prophecy, whereunto ye do well that ye take heed, as unto a light that shineth in a dark place, until the day dawn and the day-star arise in your hearts." And he told the people that this was the Scriptures, by which they were to try all doctrines, religions, and opinions. Now the Lord's power was so mighty upon me, and so strong in me, that I could not hold, but was made to cry out and say, "Oh no, it is not the Scriptures"; and I told them what it was, namely, the Holy Spirit, by which the holy men of God gave forth the Scriptures, whereby opinions, religions, and judgments were to be tried; for it led into all truth, and so gave the knowledge of all truth.

Fox's exegesis of a particular verse of Scripture was in this instance undoubtedly wrong; he was

Authority and the Light Within

young, and had much to learn; but the belief which underlay it—that the Bible is not the final authority in matters of religion, but that above the Bible is the Spirit which produced it and which enlightens every man—this was the deepest conviction of his life, and became the root principle of all his first followers, the "Children of the Light." It could be nothing but a "damnable heresy" to the ruling Protestants of the day, for it upturned the very rock on which they rested.

The early Quakers were not, for the most part, highly educated men and women, nor were they acute or logical thinkers. The ablest scholar among them was Robert Barclay, the author of the "Apology for the True Christian Divinity," whose work, though at the time it made a great impression, and was adopted as the authoritative exposition of Quaker theology, is to many modern minds, in parts at least, obscure. But these Quakers had come, like the first Christians and like Luther, into a fresh personal experience of the presence of God in their souls; and in the light of that Presence mere authoritative formulæ were as darkness. A person who can see the sun does not need either church or book to tell him of the sunshine, or of the objects it reveals to his sight. Though it was beyond their powers to frame a philosophy of the experience they enjoyed, no one who reads their writings, or studies their consistent lives and their heroism under suffering, can doubt for one moment that the experience itself was real and true. The best evidence that it was no passing exuberance of religious emotion, is the fact that on

The Authority of the Bible

the basis of that experience a church was founded, which has subsisted for two hundred and fifty years without a creed, without sacraments, and without a professional ministry.

But the early Quakers never succeeded in finding a satisfactory solution of the problem of Authority. In part their difficulty was that which the Reformed Churches had constantly had to face—the vagaries of those who professed an experience of individual illumination. The lapse of James Nayler brought them many searchings of heart. It is only just to recognise the rarity of such episodes among them, the vigour with which Nayler's proceedings were disowned, and the virtual unanimity, and consistent integrity, with which their great doctrine was upheld. But, though they always maintained that the Bible was not the final authority, in their use of the Bible they practically accepted the position of their opponents. The Spirit, they said, could never contradict Himself; hence any revelation in the present, if true, must agree with that given in the past, and might be tested by comparing it with Scripture. Here they tacitly assumed that the whole of Scripture, as we have it, was the work of the Spirit. They did not venture even as far as Luther did along the path of criticism. Barclay, indeed, shows that he understands the difficulties of the very gradual formation of the canon, of various manuscript readings, of faulty translations, and the like, so that it is very clear he does not regard the Scriptures as infallible[1]; he "sees no

---

[1] "Apology," Prop. III., "Of the Scriptures," § iv., ix.

Authority and the Light Within

necessity for believing that the Scriptures are a filled canon," recognises that there is no hard and fast line between the accepted books and the Apocrypha, and quaintly says that if "the prophecy of Enoch" should turn up, he would include it with the rest. But he does not venture to intimate that any part of the accepted Scripture is lacking in inspiration. The Epistle of James, he expressly says, may be known by the Spirit to be authentic; and apparently he regards the books of Esther and Judges as the work of the Spirit, just as much as the writings of Isaiah or of Paul.

> Moreover [he says], because they are commonly acknowledged by all to have been written by the dictates of the Holy Spirit, and that the errors which may be supposed by the injury of time to have slipped in, are not such but that there is a sufficient clear testimony left to all the essentials of the Christian faith; we do look upon them as the only fit outward judge of controversies among Christians; and that whatsoever doctrine is contrary unto their testimony may therefore justly be rejected as false. And, for our parts, we are very willing that all our doctrines and practices be tried by them.[1]

There is here a lapse of logic similar to that which led the followers of Luther and Calvin to appeal to an inward witness as the authority for just those books which Church tradition had handed down; and, just as in the Protestant churches, when faith cooled, the ambiguous position of the second generation of reformers led to the obscuration of the inward authority and the magnifying of the outward, so also it was in the Society of Friends. Its official utterances in this country, during the nineteenth century, thanks to the influence of Joseph John Gurney and others, manifest

[1] "Apology," Prop. III., § 6.

The Authority of the Bible

in large degree a return to the standard of Protestant orthodoxy.

Relatively to the other churches of the day, the position taken by the early Quakers was an enlightened one, but it could not possibly be permanently satisfying. The "testimony of the Spirit" must be understood at least as broadly as Luther understood it, if it is to put the Scriptures on a satisfactory footing. That is to say, it must include the power to test, to weigh, and if necessary to reject, that in Scripture which is of inferior spiritual quality. It must cover the right of criticism, with all that this implies. That mere moral intuition, the impression made by Scripture on the conscience, does not afford adequate ground for accepting the authority of the Bible as we have it, must surely be evident. Many parts of Scripture, indeed, like the twenty-third psalm or the Sermon on the Mount, bring with them their own authority, appealing directly to all that is best in man. But other parts make no such appeal. The imprecatory psalms, the long chronicles of bloodshed, the weary pessimism of Ecclesiastes and the fierce nationalism of Esther, are in flagrant contradiction to the gospel teachings of universal love. To attribute to them an equal authority is to substitute an external for an internal witness, to replace moral insight with an intellectual argument, to abandon spiritual discernment and deaden the moral sense.

Moreover, the "inward witness" is essentially individual, and varies with the quality and development of the reader. The writings of Paul, for example,

Authority and the Light Within

affect some spiritually-minded people more than the gospels, while others they influence less. And the same individual is "found" much more by them at one stage of his experience than at another. Some persons, of mystical and imaginative temperament, discover spiritual meanings in narratives which more prosaic minds will treat as plain matter of fact; at some periods this "spiritualising" tendency has run riot, and it has almost seemed as though, given sufficient allegorising ingenuity, anything might be made to mean anything. If Scripture is to be used (and the early Friends used it freely) as a test of doctrine, its meaning must be settled in a way that is common to all competent inquirers, and is not at the mercy of the whims of "private interpretation."

Hence it is easy to see that criticism—that is to say, historical study of the books and scientific exegesis of their contents—is absolutely necessary, if the view of the authority of the Bible held by the early Quakers, in common with the first Reformers, is to be made effective. No one is competent to say what is "the teaching of Scripture" on points of difficulty, if he uses nothing more than his own uninstructed insight, or if he has not made some study of the development of doctrines and religious conceptions in Hebrew and Jewish and early Christian times. For, as men's eyes were gradually opened, the teaching of one age differed vastly from that of another. To gain this knowledge the relative dates of the different books, and of their several parts, must be, so far as possible, ascertained, in order that ideas

The Authority of the Bible

which belong to one age may not unwittingly be attributed to another. "The testimony of the Spirit" must be broadly interpreted to cover all the light that such study can bring to a mind that is humble and sympathetic and receptive. Some would urge, in reply to this, that the use of the reason is unnecessary, on the ground that the Spirit will reveal directly all that we need to know. As Auguste Sabatier points out, this is simply to confuse the issue. The Holy Spirit does not work in such a way as to save us the trouble of using our faculties, and moral intuition does not disclose to us matters of fact.

> When from a religious impression we derive a conclusion as to the authenticity of a document, or the truth of a narrative, it is as if one were to draw from the moral impression made on him by the "Oedipus Tyrannus" of Sophocles, or Shakspeare's "Hamlet," objective and positive conclusions as to the actual history of the city of Thebes or the Kingdom of Denmark. . . . They are things of different orders, between which there is no common measure, and the questions arising in each order must be solved by essentially different processes.[1]

If it is objected that this places the interpretation of the Bible altogether out of the reach of the simple and unlearned, and makes it a matter for experts, the answer is first that the difficulty will lessen as the Bible becomes better known,[2] and second that a right understanding of theological doctrines is not necessary for beginning or maintaining the Christian life. There is enough in the New Testament that appeals, without any difficulty of interpretation, to

---

[1] A. Sabatier, "Religions of Authority," p. 182.
[2] The *translation* of the Bible is the work of experts, but their general agreement makes it available for the unlearned also. There is no reason why, in time, the same should not be true of *interpretation*.

Authority and the Light Within

the human heart and inspires the human will, to make it a priceless treasure to the most unlearned. A single Gospel, a single chapter, may bring a soul into living touch with Christ and with God. Whole pages and entire books may be obscure or misinterpreted, yet the Christian's life may be brightly burning, and may make him an efficient minister to others. Witness "Billy Bray." But, if he ventures into fields of controversy, then he must seek to equip himself to discharge worthily the task he has undertaken, and this he can only do by yielding his mind as well as his heart to the Truth of God, and seeking the testimony of the Spirit through the facts of criticism as well as through moral intuition.

If, further, the objection is raised that such inquiry as has here been indicated is needless, if not irreverent, for that Jesus Christ Himself has infallibly guaranteed the authenticity and inspiration of the books of the Old Testament, then it becomes needful to inquire more carefully into what we mean by the Authority of Christ; and this will form the subject of the next chapter.

V
THE AUTHORITY OF CHRIST

THE power of the Scriptures, which we have freely recognised, to become the channel through which the life of God may reach and vivify human hearts, must never blind us to the fact that they are human documents, each with its human history. The Inward Witness testifies to the moral beauty, the soul-reaching and heart-cleansing power, of the revelation of God that is their central theme. Religious experience in ourselves, as it deepens and broadens, verifies more and more the progressive religious experience of which the Scriptures contain the record and the expression. The Spirit within us answers to the Spirit without us; deep calls to deep.

But, as we have seen, those Protestants were guilty of grave confusion of thought, who tried to use this Inward Witness as a substitute for knowledge of history. Religious experience and insight is, indeed, an indispensable qualification for a sympathetic understanding and exposition of what the Biblical writers had to say; but, taken alone, it cannot possibly inform us how far their words have been correctly transmitted, when they lived, what were their circumstances and modes of thought, whether their writings are to be understood as history, or parable, or poetry, or what degree of credence is

Authority and the Light Within

to be attached to their statements of fact. For all these things we must use our independent powers of historical and literary study, and we must use them unhampered by conceptions of authority. The truth, and nothing else, must be both goal and guide.

There are some who fancy that this labour may be spared by an appeal to the authority of Christ Himself. While admitting, it may be, that neither Church nor Bible is the ultimate court of appeal, the attempt is made to derive an infallible authority for one or both from that of Christ. The Catholic appeals to His words to Peter (Matt. xvi. 18, 19), as implying that to him, and the Bishops of Rome as his supposed successors, was committed plenary authority in the Church. The Protestant, in the same manner, quotes His recorded utterances in regard to Noah, Jonah, Isaiah, or Daniel—or His apparent recognition of the Davidic authorship of Psalm cx.—as settling, without labour of historical inquiry, any question that might arise about them. He quotes Christ's words about the law of Moses (Matt. v. 18) as if they guaranteed the absolute Divine integrity of the Old Testament as we have it.

The position is extremely serious, for our Lord's authority is constantly being quoted to uphold positions which free and unfettered historical inquiry makes absolutely untenable. It is strange that Christians who are really loyal to Christ can commit themselves to a position of such frightful danger. To say that, if Christ is trustworthy, Moses wrote the Pentateuch or David the 110th Psalm, is to put Him

The Authority of Christ

at the mercy of the first critic who proves the contrary. And this contrary has already, by cumulative evidence, been raised to such a degree of probability as to have convinced nearly everyone whose mind is open to the facts. Without subscribing to any wild theories, every unbiassed student now recognises that there is a substantial body of real knowledge, gained by the patient labours of critics and archæologists, many of whom are sincere and reverent Christians, concerning the history of the Old Testament documents; and that this to a very large extent contradicts traditional views about them. It is sheer madness to invoke the authority of Christ to disprove the results of scientific study. One would have thought that the Church's condemnation of Galileo would have contained sufficient warning.

And, further, this use of the authority of Christ is partly a vicious circle. We use His words to prove the documents; but how do we know that we have really got His words? The inroads of criticism upon traditional views will not stop with the Old Testament; it cannot fail to be applied to the New Testament also. And it shows us that the records of Jesus did not take their present form till from thirty to forty years after His death, and only after passing through a time of oral tradition. Comparison of the same saying in different Gospels (*e.g.* Matt. v. 3 with Luke vi. 20) frequently shows how freely His sayings were rendered, how far from rigid was their form. It also gives reason to believe, especially when taken along with quotations in the early Christian writers, that

Authority and the Light Within

important doctrinal passages have been expanded or even interpolated, particularly in Matthew's Gospel.[1] Hence we can rarely press the letter of His utterances, or make much depend upon their verbal form.

It may seem to some that to admit such criticism of the Gospels is to dissolve away the figure of the Lord into pure subjectivity. These doubters surely forget that behind all criticism lie *the facts*, which neither tradition nor criticism can make or alter. And what criticism has done, and is doing, is to bring us nearer to the facts as they were: to the mind and character, the luminous and gracious personality, of the Lord Himself.

> That one Face, far from vanish, rather grows,
> Or decomposes but to recompose.

But the centre of the difficulty remains: if criticism shows that some statements which the Gospels attribute to Jesus, and which He probably made, are unbelievable, what becomes of His authority? How is it possible any longer to believe in His Divine nature? Is not the Christian faith attacked at its very heart?

To answer these questions requires a book rather than a few paragraphs[2]; and we can do no more here than indicate summarily the lines on which answers may be found. The present writer is convinced that unbiassed critical study of the Gospels and other

---

[1] *E.g.*, Matt. xvi. 18, 19; xxviii. 19.
[2] The whole subject is excellently treated by Dr. D. W. Forrest, in "The Authority of Christ." (T. and T. Clark, 1906. Price 6s.)

The Authority of Christ

early Christian writings leads inevitably to these two conclusions:—

(a) That, while His ideal of life was the highest, the mind of Jesus was wholly unclouded by any memory of conscious sin.

(b) That, while absolutely humble and dependent on the Father, He thought of Himself as the Lord and Redeemer of men.

The further conclusion to which much thought has driven him is that these facts, taken together, can only be explained on some such basis as that which finds expression in the Christology of Paul and John.[1] In these regions of thought, lying beyond the range of human experience, all that words can do is to hint at realities which they can never properly express. "The Incarnation" is one of these words. It implies (allowing for the crudities of human speech) that some portion or aspect of the Divine nature became embodied in an actual human life as the man Jesus of Nazareth. "Being in the form of God, He emptied Himself, and was found in the likeness of men." "The Word became flesh, and dwelt among us."

If this is so, then the authority of Christ, as the eternal Word, is no other than the authority of God Himself, and is therefore final and absolute. So much we fully grant. But this is not to attribute Divine

[1] Auguste Sabatier, in the work we have frequently quoted, puts this conclusion aside. While there is much in his presentation of the Christian life that must appeal profoundly to every spiritually minded person, he appears in his central thought to get somewhat away from the facts. The essence of the Gospel, he says, is to produce in us a consciousness of "inward reconciliation with God, identical with that of Jesus" ("Religions of Authority," p. 274). Was the consciousness of Jesus really one of *reconciliation* with God?

Authority and the Light Within

infallibility to every word He is reported to have spoken in the body, or even to every thought that passed through His human mind. His words, as we have seen, come to us through history, and are therefore necessarily subject to criticism; and His thoughts while in the flesh were dependent on His *humanity*, and were therefore compassed with limitation. The Incarnation does not, any more than Church or Bible, provide us with an infallible *outward* authority.

We are aware that, in saying this, we traverse certain opinions known as orthodox, which have embodied themselves in some of the great creeds of Christendom. This is because we are convinced that the orthodox creeds, while nominally maintaining at once the divinity and humanity of Jesus, have in effect thrown the latter away. That is to say, they have tried to combine it with the divinity in such a way as to render His personality at once inconceivable and contrary to the facts.

In order that our discussion may be as concrete as possible, let us confine it to one point: *did Jesus know everything?* The usual orthodox answer is that, as He was God, of course He did. But, as Dr. Forrest says ("Authority of Christ," p. 57), those who thus draw abstract conclusions from the Deity of Jesus are apt to lose sight altogether of the very facts out of which belief in His Deity arose. All the facts in the Gospels lead to an opposite conclusion. Jesus frankly owned there were some most important things He did not know (Mark xiii. 32). He grew in wisdom as well as in stature (Luke ii. 52); He marvelled at

The Authority of Christ

the unbelief of His people (Mark vi. 6); He asked questions, for information, like anyone else (Mark vi. 38).

There are those who have tried to cover these facts by supposing that Jesus, as God, knew things which, as man, He did not know. This is to say in words what is to thought an absolute contradiction, and is therefore unthinkable; it is also entirely contrary to the evidence we have. It implies that there was, in Jesus, a double consciousness; in fact, that there were in Him two persons. Now, of this there is not one trace on the pages of the Gospels. The personality they reveal to us is, indeed, far beyond our power to fathom; but, so far as we can pierce its depths, it is perfectly transparent, simple, and harmonious. The divine nature is not something *added to* the human nature; it is something *in* the human nature, which the perfection of the latter forces us to recognise. "God was in Christ."[1]

The only way by which we can be true to our own thought, and also to the New Testament, is to admit that the Son of God, in taking our nature upon Him, laid aside some of the attributes of Deity, in order that He might accomplish the work that was given Him, by manifesting to the full the one essential attribute which He did not lay aside—His love. We

---

[1] The misfortune of the old theology was that it started with God and man as two wholly separate natures, "pole-wide apart"; and it sought to solve the impossible problem how these two could be combined in a single person. We are learning that man in his true nature is not a being wholly separate from God, but that they are essentially "conjunct." (See Rufus Jones, "The Double Search," pp. 30, 31.)

Authority and the Light Within

shall admit at once that He put from Him His omnipresence; probably we include omnipotence. Why should we draw the line here, and refuse to include omniscience? If we do so, we lose, whatever we may say, His true humanity. For a real man is one who learns, who grows, in mind as well as in body: an omniscient baby is not a human child. Yet, if Jesus of Nazareth was not omniscient in His cradle, at what point did He become so?

The truth is, that it is only as we recognise the *Kenosis*, or "self-emptying," spoken of by Paul (Phil. ii. 7), as an essential element in the Incarnation, that we can really believe in it, or be faithful to the facts we find, or understand, as fully as we are meant to do, the depth of the Divine sacrifice on man's behalf. The Atonement found its consummation in the Cross, but it did not begin there. "God so loved the world, that He gave His only-begotten Son."

The Son of God, for our redemption from sin, submitted Himself to become one of us. He became our brother: a real man, a real Jew, fulfilling indeed the highest of His people's yearnings, yet sharing many of their limitations. He knew nothing of Greek philosophy or Roman law; poetry and art and science were beyond His ken. But He steeped Himself in His nation's sacred literature; and, while transcending the religious ideas of His time, He spoke, and doubtless thought, according to the fashion of His day. The scheme of the universe which His people held, He held also. To teach them a better astronomy was no part of the work He had come to do; and literary

The Authority of Christ

and historical criticism lay equally outside His sphere. He took these things as He found them; to have done otherwise would have hindered His purpose of revealing the Father and redeeming men from sin to the life of God. The more clearly we discern His purpose, and the more firmly we hold to it, the more unfettered will be our freedom of inquiry into matters of history.

The authority of the human Christ, then, differs not in nature but only in degree from that of all who can see more deeply than others into the truth of things. Everyone, as was said in the first chapter of this book, who has special first-hand knowledge on any subject, speaks about it with authority, and that authority is recognised. The prophets and saints of humanity have authority when they tell us what they see of the deep things of God and of the spiritual life of man. Their authority is relative and partial, but it is none the less real. So the authority with which Jesus of Nazareth speaks of God, of sin, of forgiveness and of righteousness, is a part of that wondrous clearness of spiritual vision which shines everywhere on the Gospel pages, and which can only have been possible for One who lived ever in perfect communion with God. His authority covers the matters of which He had special knowledge, not those of which He had not. To quote His words in support of traditional theories of the Old Testament is to miss His true significance, to go back from the light and freedom of the Gospel to the darkness and bondage of the Scribes and Pharisees.

Authority and the Light Within

Admittedly the work of Christ was only begun, not finished, while He was here on earth. "I have yet many things to say unto you, but ye cannot bear them now. Howbeit when he, the Spirit of truth, is come, he shall guide you into all the truth" (John xvi. 12, 13). We hope in the next chapter to show how, through the Spirit, the authority of Christ became effective for the direction of His Church.

VI

THE AUTHORITY OF THE SPIRIT

It has often been remarked that the Apostolic writers make but little use of the deeds and sayings of Jesus, as recorded in the Gospels. Whether we take the New Testament epistles, or the pictures of early Christian preaching given us in the Acts of the Apostles, the references to the acts or words of the Master are surprisingly few. His birth into our human nature—His death for our sins—His resurrection by which "life and immortality" were "brought to light"—are almost the only events in His career that are ever mentioned. And very rarely are His teachings quoted as authoritative, even when we should expect them to be inevitably appealed to as the final court of reference.

This fact has been used to throw doubt upon the historicity of the Gospel narratives, and even upon the historic existence of Jesus Himself. We are convinced that that is a mistaken inference, for the simple reason that without Jesus behind them the first Christians are absolutely inexplicable—they are simply an event without a cause, a greater miracle than orthodoxy itself has ever dreamed of.

Nevertheless the fact is a strange one, and demands explanation. It is not enough to say, what is perfectly true, that, when Paul wrote most of his Epistles,

Authority and the Light Within

the Gospels, as we have them, were not yet compiled. For it is practically certain that, from the time of the departure of Jesus, stories of His deeds, and collections of His sayings, had been carefully taught and handed on from mouth to mouth. It is these that form the basis of our first three Gospels; the material was certainly at hand for Paul to use, had he so desired.[1]

The absence of reference to the word of the Master is perhaps most striking in the settlement of the hardest question His first followers had to face— the position of converted Gentiles in the new society, and the authority over them (and, indeed, over Christians generally) of the Mosaic law. The passages that throw light upon the acute controversy which arose about this question are Paul's Epistle to the Galatians (chapters i. to v.), and Acts xi. 1-18, xv. 1-29. In the whole of this there is only one reference to any word of Jesus (Acts xi. 16).

No doubt, even if these disciples had wished to do so, it would not have been easy to settle their difficulty by reference to the actual sayings of their Master. If one party quoted the prophecy that "Many shall come from the east and from the west and shall sit down in the Kingdom of heaven" (Matt. viii. 11), others could remind them of the words, "I was not sent but unto the lost sheep of the house of Israel" (Matt. xv. 24), and "Go not into any way of the Gentiles" (Matt. x. 5). If some pleaded His freedom from

---

[1] In Acts xx. 35, Paul is reported as quoting, from this floating tradition, the saying (not elsewhere recorded): "It is more blessed to give than to receive."

The Authority of the Spirit

any strictness of Sabbatic observance—or the boldness with which, in declaring that "nothing from without can defile a man" (Mark vii. 15, 19), he "made all meats clean," and set aside much of the ceremonial law—others could reply that He had declared, "One jot or one tittle shall in no wise pass from the law, till all things be accomplished" (Matt. v. 18). His method of teaching did not easily lend itself to mechanical reference, as to an authoritative standard.

Nothing is more remarkable than to notice the contrast between these disciples and the Jewish scribes. The scribes decided every question by quoting some authority—a precept in their sacred law, with the interpretation and application laid down by this Rabbi or by that. The disciples of Jesus, while using with freedom the prophetic writings, scarcely ever quote their own Master. For this there must be some reason, which the occasional, and often paradoxical, character of His utterances does not fully yield. What the reason was may be gathered from that one quotation which Peter does make in Acts xi. 16: "*Ye shall be baptized with the Holy Ghost.*" It was because they had a present illumination that they did not need to seek it in the past; because of their daily experience of a living and accessible Guide that they never cast back their eyes regretfully to those three sinless years, as to a time when the will of God had been more clearly known.

The reference of these Christians is not to the

Authority and the Light Within

spoken words of Jesus, but to the mind of the Spirit. "It seemed good to the Holy Ghost and to us" (Acts xv. 28); they were "forbidden of the Holy Ghost to speak the word in Asia" (xvi. 6). The experience of divine control and direction was not confined to a favoured few; it was the normal endowment of all who genuinely accepted Jesus Christ. Indeed, it was this gift and nothing else that constituted a Christian. It was because the Holy Ghost had "fallen on" Cornelius and his friends that Peter judged them to be fit for baptism (Acts x. 44-48). " As many as are led by the Spirit of God, these are sons of God" (Rom. viii. 14).[1]

In all ages the sorest of human problems has been the "Silence of God." The hunger of the human soul for a voice from heaven—for some clear knowledge of the hidden mind of God—is seen not alone in the resort, in ancient days, to inspired prophets and priests with their Urim and Thummim, but in Delphic oracle and Roman augury, in magic and divination, in the persistent belief, wide as the human race, that certain persons had dealings with the unseen world. See how the first Christians believed that this world-hunger was satisfied.

In the Book of Acts the chief disciple of Jesus is represented as claiming the gift of the Spirit as evidence that the Messianic age has come—for that the prophecy of Joel has been now fulfilled, that Divine inspiration shall no longer be the privilege

[1] See Sabatier, "Religions of Authority," pp. 301—305; Forrest, "Authority of Christ," pp. 351—360.

The Authority of the Spirit

of the few, but shall be poured out upon all flesh (Acts ii. 15-18). The gift of the prophet—direct access to God and clear intimations of His mind and will—had now been made the gift of servants and of handmaidens, of every humblest believer in Jesus. *The Christian Church was founded as the Church of an inspired people.*

What was "the Spirit," how were its intimations received, and what was the nature of its authority?

In the first place, it was regarded as continuous with the source of inspiration of prophets and psalmists (Acts i. 16), as the Divine power that filled the Master Himself (Acts x. 38), and with which He baptized His followers. But, in the second place, it was in some sense a *new* gift, being identified with His own personality, risen and exalted. "The Spirit was not yet," wrote the author of the fourth Gospel, "because Jesus was not yet glorified" (John vii. 39). "I will not leave you orphans," he reports Jesus as saying, "I come unto you" (John xiv. 18). "They assayed to go into Bithynia, but the Spirit of Jesus suffered them not" (Acts xvi. 7).[1]

The two thoughts of the Spirit as continuous, and of the Spirit as a new gift, were harmonised in the

---

[1] Expressions like the above show that we cannot rightly interpret the Apostles' language by trying to make it fit the mould of a definitely formulated creed, such as that of the "three Persons" of the Trinity. That doctrine is a theory, devised much later, to explain apostolic thoughts, which, when uttered, did not run on systematic lines. We cannot, without greatly misrepresenting them, show that the Apostles uniformly spoke of one set of spiritual functions being discharged by Christ, another by the Spirit, and so on. Note the identification, in Rom. viii. 9, 10, of "The Spirit of God," "The Spirit of Christ" and "Christ."

Authority and the Light Within

Johannine theology by the doctrine of the Word made flesh. The eternal Divine Word had always been with men, as a "light that lighteth every man," a "life" in which men found their "light." But now, in the last days, this diffused light had been, as it were, concentrated into the full blaze of the person of Jesus Christ. He left this world only to return again in the Spirit—no longer, as in former days, a dimly perceived influence, but recognised now as a personal presence, the same living and active personality who, as Jesus of Nazareth, had lived and died for men.[1]

The authority of Christ, then, was applied by the first Christians, not through any mechanical appeal to the letter of His words on earth, but by seeking and following the teaching of His Spirit in their hearts. They do not appear to have regarded the presence of the Spirit as something wholly "miraculous," whose working would be hindered by the use of their ordinary faculties of reason and judgment. It was largely through the right use of these faculties that the Spirit taught them—largely from facts and circumstances that they gathered what the mind of the Spirit was. Chief among these new facts was one that greatly disconcerted them—the evidence that Christ was working outside the barriers of Jewish law and practice. They had their choice to open their minds to these new facts, or to close them and continue in the old, narrow groove. They chose the better path, submitted themselves to the facts, and found their hearts enlarged and their

[1] See further Chapters XIII. and XIV., especially pages 116, 121.

The Authority of the Spirit

spiritual vision quickened. Their own inward experience was verified in the changed lives all around them, in the fellowship of those who, with them, were walking in the light.

> We have here [says Dr. Forrest] a classical illustration of what is meant by the illumination of the Spirit, and of the methods of His operation. In their whole action the one concern of the Apostles was to be loyal to the purpose of their Master. They had the most vivid recollection of the time when He was with them, and of the teaching that He had imparted to them. But where His word or example was insufficient for present guidance, they never doubted that fresh light would break for them. They found the sure indications of His mind through submitting themselves to His discipline of their life. What they had imagined to be primary and essential in His utterances or acts, they now perceived to be subordinate or temporary. They read His declarations with a new accent or emphasis; and they did so confidently, because it was still He who was teaching them by His Spirit.

It was not only the collective Church that was thus taught by the Spirit, but the same divine illumination was known in measure by each true Christian, however humble. "The young men saw visions and the old men dreamed dreams." Yet this made none of them infallible, not even the greatest. They record, in the frankest manner, their disagreements. Paul reproached Peter at Antioch, "because he stood condemned," and quarrelled with his beloved Barnabas on the question of a companion. He gave up his confident belief in the early return of his Master, yet never doubted that he had had the Spirit. He frequently, in his writings, utters warnings against the spirit of infallibility, and this usually in close connection with assurances of the fulness of the Spirit's power. If his readers were to be "filled unto all the

Authority and the Light Within

fulness of God," they must also " walk in all lowliness and meekness, forbearing one another in love"; if "filled with the Spirit," they must yet "subject themselves one to another in the fear of Christ."[1] Inspired preachers at Corinth must keep themselves under control, and be willing to yield one to another, that all things might be done decently and in order.[2]

The authority of the Spirit, as Paul conceives it, is therefore the authority of the living Christ, present and available for His sincere, obedient, and humble followers. But the Spirit is not something wholly miraculous, wholly foreign to their own true nature, which makes any of them into infallible oracles of God. It is, in truth, their own best nature. God in them is the fulfilment of the best they have it in them to become. The higher nature begotten in them is the "first-fruits of the Spirit," with promise of ever richer fruition. The "groanings which cannot be uttered," with which the Spirit "comes in on our behalf," are identical with the groanings that we ourselves utter in the longing for a fuller experience of God (Rom. viii. 23-27).

And so the Light Within is the light of God as we allow Him to become one with us.

[1] Eph. iii. 14—iv. 4 ; v. 18-21.
[2] 1 Cor. xiv. 29-33.

VII

WHAT IS THE LIGHT WITHIN?

In the first chapter the attempt was made to set forth the nature of Authority; and the conclusion was reached that all Authority, except that of God Himself, is limited and relative. Authority, it was pointed out, has necessarily a large part to play in controlling the thoughts and deeds of men, for the reason that we are not isolated units, but are largely dependent on, and moulded by, the society in which we find ourselves. And yet society itself can only prosper if the individuals that compose it have free scope to develop their personality; so that the true function of Authority is gradually to efface itself—to make itself needless by preparing the way for the Autonomy of the individual. Parents and teachers must endeavour to train children to obey the right from choice, not from compulsion, and to learn truth for themselves by independent examination of the facts. This "autonomy of the individual," it was urged, is something wholly different from lawless self-assertion; it is inward consecration to truth and goodness; and, since truth is one and goodness is also one, the right development of autonomy produces not chaos, but order and harmony.

Passing from the general field of thought and life to that which is regarded as specifically religious, and in

Authority and the Light Within

which the claim of Authority to rule the thoughts and deeds of men has been most insistent, we examined one by one the infallible outward authorities that men have set up, and found that none of them could make good its claim to an absolute and final dominion. Provisionally, and as teachers, they will have a large and rightful place, but it will always be as training us for the use of our own original powers of spiritual perception. We shall not presumptuously expect to be saved the trouble of the search for God, either on the one hand by having Truth infallibly dealt out to us at second-hand, or on the other by having it miraculously revealed to us *de novo*, without any effort on our part to enter into the larger spiritual experience which the race has accumulated. We shall humbly make use of the authorities around us, remembering that their work is to train us for spiritual autonomy, in order that the light without us may become a Light Within.

The most difficult part of our task now awaits us—to gain, if we may, some clear thoughts upon the nature and the working of this Inward Witness. It is and must be difficult, because it involves the most intimate relations between the human and the Divine. It is vain to fancy that the writer of these articles, or anyone else, can so clear up the matter that there will be no further trouble in understanding it. These deep spiritual realities are not subjects for rounded and finished demonstration, like propositions in geometry. Even in outward nature there are depths beyond depths, and it is only our surface

What is the Light Within?

experiences that can be expressed in precise and accurate language. Tennyson declared, of the "flower in the crannied wall," that, if he understood it completely, he would "know what God and man is." Much more are we likely to be baffled in trying to convey to one another, by the agency of human speech, the truth we may have discerned of those deep realities that lie behind the veil.

At least, however, it may be possible to clear away some of the mists that have hung around this subject through the use of a worn-out philosophy, and because of the different conceptions which the phrase "the Light Within" has been made to cover. Taking the second point first, as being the easier, we may distinguish at least four meanings that have been attached to the words. If the subject is dealt with, for the present, in purely human terms, it is that we may make the safer progress by advancing "from the known to the unknown."

(a) "The Light Within" has been used, as above suggested, to distinguish a personal and individual apprehension of truth from a belief resting on authority. It is, however, inappropriate to use it in regard to matters of ordinary sense knowledge. If someone tells me he has found a primrose with eleven petals, and I refuse to credit it until I have seen the specimen, I should not think of dignifying the demonstration with the title of a "light within." It is when we come to the deeper and more hidden objects of thought, which can never become objects of sense perception, that the phrase is more legitimately used.

Authority and the Light Within

Anyone, for instance, who can fathom and expound convincingly a great work of genius, like one of Shakspeare's plays, might be said to reach his conviction of the meaning by a "light within." He uses the deeper experiences of his life, of which he may be only partly conscious, to interpret what he finds. Still more appropriate would it be, when the object of study is a real person, to say that one's apprehension of his true character is given by an inner light. Deep answers to deep, beyond what words can convey or clear thought formulate. Authority may prepare the way for it,—we may "hear of him by the hearing of the ear"; but it is when our "eye seeth him," when we come into personal relations, that we gain an assured conviction of his character which no words from another can either give or take away.

(*b*) "The Light Within" has also been used, more restrictedly, with reference to our perception of *moral* truth: that is, our power to distinguish right from wrong, together with the consciousness that we "ought" to pursue the one and avoid the other. Whether this power is "innate," or a product of race experience, we need not now discuss. All that concerns us is to show that, as it exists in the individual, it is an "inward" and not an "outward" light: it is not given by the facts but through the person. No amount of observation of *what is* will ever give the sense of *what ought to be*. The possession of a moral ideal, however imperfectly conceived and however feebly adhered to, is something entirely different from

What is the Light Within?

knowledge of the outward world; there is a witness "within" us that testifies to its truth.

(c) Again, the phrase has been still further narrowed to express not so much our ethical perception in general, as the sense of individual duty in particulars. The consciousness of a special "call" to do one thing or to refrain from another, beyond what we can give a clear reason for, is probably in some form universal among those who are concerned to do right. There is probably no one who strives to make the best of his life but has a sense that some particular line of work is marked out for him—that he has, as Mazzini used to say, in some sort a "mission." In some persons there is much more than this. Socrates was conscious of a "daimon" which warned him against wrong steps; multitudes of Christians, and some who would not claim that name, have sought and found a Guidance in detail for themselves individually. The clearness with which these "monitions" come differs enormously, even among persons of equally devoted life; to some they are like the earthquake and the whirlwind, to others like the still small voice. But, in whatever way there comes this sense of individual duty, it is a "Light Within," a degree of personal illumination.

(d) Lastly, the phrase "The Light Within" finds its most appropriate usage in reference to our knowledge of God, and of life in relation to Him. This we may speak of, broadly, as "divine truth." As we shall see, it is not really a separate region, rigidly marked off from other truth. But what has been said above as

Authority and the Light Within

to the perception of spiritual truth and goodness applies here *a fortiori*. God is the deepest foundation of all truth, the highest ideal of all goodness. He is not one impressive phenomenon among other phenomena, one mighty fact among other facts. He is the reality of which phenomena are but appearances, the basis of the difference we make between truth and falsehood, and the ground of all our moral distinctions. Sense knowledge, and the inferences we base upon it, will never reach Him. Our telescopes may peer into the depths of space, our microscopes may search after the very molecules of the brain, our reasonings show that each molecule is a complex world; but none of these discoveries can bring us one single step nearer God.

Hence, if we are to have any knowledge of Him, it must be "from within"; it must come to us, like our knowledge of character and goodness, through something that is in ourselves.[1] We may reason as we will of "natural theology"—and such reasonings, rightly conducted, may lead us to the gateway of divine truth; but until the gate opens, and God manifests Himself to our inner consciousness, we shall not really know Him. The same may be said of teaching about God, and beliefs about Him. We may study

[1] It is, of course, true that all knowledge whatever "comes to us through something in ourselves." We know the world only as it relates itself to consciousness. But we do not know God only "as He relates Himself to consciousness," for He *is* consciousness—the supreme and universal consciousness. Our knowledge of God is closely akin to our knowledge of ourselves. It is because people find out that the knowledge of God is not sense knowledge, but have not yet discovered what it is, that they fancy it is not *real* knowledge and so become atheists or agnostics.

What is the Light Within?

Scripture and recite the Creeds; but these are dull and cold till the day comes when they glow with an inward light—when they are no longer mere words but represent *realities*, felt and experienced in the depths of our inmost soul.[1]

If the above analysis is sound, it follows that the Light Within is possessed, in some measure, by every self-conscious and reasoning being, by everyone who is truly *a person*. It also follows that the measure of the Light, the clearness with which it shines, depends very greatly on the person: not alone upon his "natural" endowment, but upon the extent to which he himself has lived in and obeyed it.

In the following chapters it is proposed to examine and to criticise the doctrine of "The Light Within" as it was formulated by the early Quakers, and after that to attempt to set forth its true nature as something which is both divine and human, including its relations to Reason and to Conscience, and to that in Christianity which makes it distinctively "the Religion of the Spirit."

[1] This is set forth with greater fulness in the following chapter.

VIII

THE QUAKERS ON THE LIGHT WITHIN

THE Society of Friends was founded upon belief in Immediate Revelation. Quakerism was, essentially, as has been previously said, "the appeal from a dead to a living God—from one whose word was a fossil, stored carefully in a museum, to one who still spoke and breathed in the hearts of living men."[1] It was not the result of psychological analysis or philosophic speculation; it sprang neither from the cloister nor from the university; it was the outcome of the spiritual struggles of a half-educated shepherd lad, who, in a desperate soul-conflict with darkness, and without help from the religious professors of his day, found light and peace from the voice of "One, even Christ Jesus, who could speak to his condition." It had much in common with the mysticism of Anabaptists and others, who carried further than Luther and Calvin had dared to carry it the revolt against Authority which we call the Reformation, and who alleged that a light from God was in them, superior to any that could be borrowed at second-hand from the Scriptures of the past. What saved it from degenerating into "the anarchy of the Ranters" was the sobriety of character, the intense moral earnestness, and the sound common-sense, which in George Fox

[1] See Chapter IV., p. 37.

The Quakers on the Light Within

were associated with mystical enthusiasm. While undoubtedly his religion had its attraction for "cranks" and fanatics, yet among those who were drawn to Fox, who were dissatisfied with the aridity of much of the Puritan preaching, and who found for themselves the same inward light and richness of experience that he enjoyed, were some of the sanest and strongest spirits that Puritanism had produced.

It was said above that Quakerism was founded on the conviction of immediate revelation. That is to say, the early Friends with one voice maintained that it was only by the operation of something Divine in a man that God could become real to him, that the Scriptures could be understood, or that he could have any true perception of moral truth or individual duty. This is what they meant by "the Light Within," and this was the root of all their preaching. Penn says of Fox :—

> In his testimony on ministry, he much laboured to open truth to the people's understandings, and to bottom them upon the principle, Christ Jesus, the Light of the world, that by bringing them to something that was of God in themselves, they might the better know and judge of Him and themselves.[1]

Fox himself is perfectly clear in his statements that a measure of this Light is given to all, and not to any favoured few :—

> Now the Lord God opened to me by his invisible power "that every man was enlightened by the Divine light of Christ"; and I saw it shine through all; and that they that believed in it came out of condemnation to the light of life, and became the children of it; but they that hated it, and did not believe in it, were condemned by it, though they made a profession of Christ. This I saw in the pure openings of the light,

[1] William Penn; Preface to George Fox's "Journal," p. xlvii.

Authority and the Light Within

without the help of any man; neither did I then know where to find it in the Scriptures, though afterwards, searching the Scriptures, I found it. For I saw, in that Light and Spirit which was before the Scriptures were given forth, and which led the holy men of God to give them forth, that all must come to that Spirit if they would know God, or Christ, or the Scriptures aright, which they that gave them forth were led and taught by.[1]

The substance of Fox's preaching is indicated by himself, when he says, " I declared to them how that God was come to teach His people Himself, and to bring them off from all their man-made teachers to hear His Son."[2] With this agree the words of Barclay:—

Glory to God for ever! who hath chosen us as first-fruits to himself in this day, wherein he is arisen to plead with the nations; and therefore hath sent us forth to preach this everlasting gospel unto all, Christ nigh to all, the light in all, the seed sown in the hearts of all, that men may come and apply their minds to it.[3]

The outward knowledge of Christ and of the teaching of the Bible was not undervalued by the early Friends; but they steadily maintained that *some* knowledge, at least, of God was possible without it,[4] and that the outward knowledge did not, without direct revelation in the heart, give the real knowledge. Barclay and the others insist that there is a wide difference, in our apprehension of God and of life in relation to Him, between theoretical and experimental

---

[1] Fox's "Journal," 8th Ed., 1901, pp. 34, 35.
[2] *Ibid.*, p. 48.
[3] Barclay, "Apology," Prop. vi., § 24.
[4] It appears to the present writer that most of them were inclined to over-estimate the knowledge of God and of "divine truth" possessed by those we call the heathen; but their position was far nearer to the truth than that of their opponents, who virtually denied such knowledge altogether.

The Quakers on the Light Within

knowledge—between knowledge *about* these things and knowledge *of* the things themselves.[1]

> We do distinguish between the certain knowledge of God, and the uncertain; between the spiritual knowledge, and the literal; the saving heart-knowledge, and the soaring head-knowledge. The last, we confess, may be divers ways obtained; but the first, by no other way than the inward immediate manifestation and revelation of God's Spirit, shining in and upon the heart, enlightening and opening the understanding.[2]

There is, surely, a deep truth in these expressions, which the world is far from having fully apprehended. Teachings about God, reasonings about His being and nature, can do no more than prepare the way for the true knowledge, which can only come from His direct touch upon our souls. "I have heard of thee by the hearing of the ear, but now mine eye seeth thee." True religion is quite other than acceptance of opinions or beliefs, or even of a code of laws believed to have come from God; it is an experience and a life. So long as it is merely taken at second-hand from other men, or is thought of as a mechanical obedience—so long as it reaches no witness of truth deep in the soul—it is not religion at all, but, at best, only what Paul called a "tutor."[3]

There is something in the consciousness of God which everyone who has, however dimly, entered into it, knows to be the best and highest thing that life has to give. It yields an assurance of reality, which

---

[1] Royce illustrates this distinction by the difference between a *description* of my hat and the *feeling* of it on my own head.
[2] Barclay, "Apology," Prop. ii., § 1.
[3] Gal. iii. 24: "The law hath been our *paidagōgos* to bring us to Christ."

Authority and the Light Within

on the one hand is far removed from mere emotional excitement, and which, on the other, no intellectual process, by itself, can either give or take away.

> Whoso has felt the Spirit of the Highest
> Cannot confound nor doubt Him nor deny;
> Yea, with one voice, O world, though thou deniest,
> Stand thou on that side, for on this am I.[1]

All really spiritual teachers recognise that there is this first-hand, intuitional, or revelational element in the perception of religious truth—that our power to perceive depends mainly on what we are, on how we have used and are using the inward light we have. Says Herrmann:—

We have not found God until He rules in our inner life. . . . We have God just in so far as He Himself comes near to us. . . . We must regard as revelation only that which brings us into actual communion with God; and we can regard as the thoughts of our own faith only what comes home to us as truth within the sphere of our actual communion. Thus all that can be the object of Christian doctrine is summed up in religious experience.[2]

And Auguste Sabatier:—

To be a Christian is not to acquire a notion of God, or even an abstract doctrine of His paternal love; it is to live over, within ourselves, the inner spiritual life of Christ, and by the union of our heart with His to *feel* in ourselves the presence of a Father and the reality of our filial relation to Him. It is not a question of a new teaching, but of a transformed consciousness.[3]

Again, a recent writer says:—

If God Himself spoke or tried to speak to one who was not ready to anticipate and interpret His message by a life of Godward effort, the message would of necessity remain unspoken; for in the atmosphere of commonplace thought and feeling even the largest and loftiest words

---
[1] F. W. H. Myers, "St. Paul."
[2] "Communion with God," pp. 30, 31, 37.
[3] "Religions of Authority," etc., pp. 293, 294.

The Quakers on the Light Within

become unfit, as unfit as are the symbols of mathematics, for the transmission of divine truth.[1]

It is not only Christians who have recognised this truth; Maurice Maeterlinck would probably not call himself a Christian at all, yet he writes:—

> It is not by telling yourself that God is great, and that you move in His radiance, that you will be able to live in the beauty and fertile depths where the heroes dwelt. You may, perhaps, remind yourself, day and night, that the hands of all the invisible powers are waving over your head like a tent with countless folds, and yet shall the least gesture of these hands be imperceptible to you. It behoves you to be keenly vigilant; better had you watch in the market place than slumber in the temple.[2]

And this is surely what the Master Himself meant when He said that only "the pure in heart shall see God;" that if the inward "eye be single, thy whole body shall be full of light." He gave a blessing to Peter, for that it was not flesh and blood, but the Father in heaven, who had revealed to him the divine character of his Teacher,[3] and declared that it was those alone who loved Him and kept His commandments, to whom He could make Himself manifest.[4] The fourth Gospel is full of the thought that a Light from God has been given to all men, and that it is as they obey this light, and follow it, that they will be led to receive the fuller light that shines in the "Word made flesh."[5] This is what Paul meant when he said that "the natural man receiveth not the things

---

[1] "The Creed of Christ," p. 71.
[2] "The Treasure of the Humble."
[3] Matt. xvi. 17.
[4] John xiv. 21.
[5] John i. 4, 9; iii. 19-21; v. 17; vi. 44, 45; xii. 32, etc. See further Chapter XIII., pp. 116-119.

Authority and the Light Within

of the Spirit of God," because they are to be "spiritually judged."[1]

The discovery of the early Quakers was, then, essentially, that *there is something of God in every person*—a little piece, as it were, of the Infinite.[2] It was a perception of the Divine immanence, which brought back the heavenly Voice from the past to the present, found the Revelation of God not closed but continuous, and made religion consist in His expanding life in the soul, instead of an intellectual assent to a system of doctrines about Him. It meant that, as men's eyelids open to the daylight, their knowledge of Truth is always growing, and cannot be finally petrified in any formula. In Quakerism Christianity reverted to its Apostolic essence—*a new way of living*, in touch with the realised person of Christ—and was no longer a claim to acquittal at the bar of God, on the ground of accepting certain doctrines. So far from salvation being something finished and completed, it was a life capable of infinite expansion—boundless in its possibilities of growth and blessedness—accepting no lower standard than that of being "perfect, even as the Father which is in heaven is perfect."

All this, and much more, was contained in the discovery of "the Light Within." Many of the doctrines of Christianity remained, for those who became

---
[1] 1 Cor. ii. 14.
[2] Personality is self-consciousness; and it can be shown psychologically that self-consciousness involves something of infinitude. (See Royce, in "Hibbert Journal," October, 1902). It is not a contradiction to say that something of infinitude can co-exist with the finite; a surface, for instance, may be infinitely long but of finite breadth.

The Quakers on the Light Within

Quakers, much as before; when challenged, they tried to formulate their creed very much in the orthodox manner. It was what they did with the doctrines, where they placed them, that made the chief difference between them and their Puritan persecutors. "*You*," says Isaac Penington, "lay stress upon a notion; the Lord hath brought *me* into a life, which I live by the springing up of life in me." " In the Light I meet with assurance. . . . He creates a new heart in me, which is spirit like [the Light] itself." It follows that for those who became really Quakers, however they might express their faith, Christianity could never again be tied down to a system of dogmatic formulæ: truth was infinitely expansive; a breath was in it as of the infinite sea.

What weaknesses there were, in the presentation of their discovery, we must glance at in the next chapter.

IX

THE WEAKNESS OF QUAKERISM[1]

THE central discovery of the Quakers was, as we have seen, the truth of Immediate Revelation. They believed in it because it had come to them; they were "Children of the Light" not because they had read about it in a book, but because they had entered into the Light and it shone upon them. And this experience, which transformed their lives, they were assured might be known by *all* who would but seek it and obey. A measure of the same Light was given to all men, and would, if followed faithfully, lead into the fulness of day. In each soul something of God was present, something by which He was seeking to reveal Himself.

We cannot doubt that in this experience, and in the largeness of outlook that came with it, the early Friends struck the true and final basis of spiritual religion. It was an assurance of the Divine immanence: "something of God in every person": and, as we have seen, it brought religion back from a creed to a life, finding its essence no longer in "a notion," but in an experience. It did not disparage

[1] The writer desires to acknowledge his indebtedness, in this and the preceding and following chapters, to Dr. Rufus M. Jones for thoughts contained in lectures given at the Friends' Summer School at Bakewell (August, 1906), and also for some quotations from the writings of the early Friends.

The Weakness of Quakerism

the Bible, or the work on earth of Jesus Christ; but it affirmed that neither could be truly known through teaching by voice or book, without an inward revelation from the Spirit.

The depth and reality of the experience that brought light to the souls of these early Quakers is evidenced by the sober consistency of their lives, by their heroic endurance of persecution, and by the fact that they were able to found a religious society which, with neither priest nor sacrament nor liturgy, has produced and nourished saintly souls, and has endured for two hundred and fifty years. Yet, when we examine the attempts they made to formulate what they had discovered, we find weaknesses which have undoubtedly hindered the acceptance by the world of their message. The weakness is most apparent when they are most anxious to fit their scheme of thought into the frame which was regarded as "orthodox." They are strong in their appeal to inward experience; weak in their endeavours, by formal statement, to guard themselves against theological attacks.

The Friends produced no philosopher, and no poet till the nineteenth century. No leader arose among them to do what Paul did for the early Church—no man whose commanding intellect, added to profound religious insight, gave him a range and sweep of thought that could put things in their true perspective, and, taking the ideas of the time, both old and new, sift the permanent from the temporary. Their only theologian, Robert Barclay, did his work at the age of

Authority and the Light Within

twenty-eight, and his "Apology" was soon accepted as an authoritative presentment of Quakerism.

A little study of the "Apology" reveals to a modern reader the centre of weakness. Barclay and the other early Quakers did their thinking in terms of their own age; for them as for other Christians of the seventeenth century the world was *an unmixed dualism*. The "natural" and the "spiritual" stood confronting one another but never mingling; God and the world were separated by an unbridged chasm. George Fox records an experience in which the thought came to him that "all things come by Nature"; and this, he clearly implies, was for him equivalent to the suggestion that "there is no God."[1] Moreover, they never thought of doubting the truth, as literal history, of the Fall of Man recorded in Genesis, or of questioning the deductions drawn from it by the theology of their day. For them, as for the most rigid Calvinist, man was absolutely lost and ruined by the Fall. No spark of a higher nature remained to him; his whole being was, just so far as human, totally and hopelessly corrupt and evil.[2] The

---

[1] See "Journal," Vol. I. p. 26 (Ed. 1901).
[2] See Barclay, "Apology," Prop. iv., § 1: "We cannot suppose that men, who are come of Adam naturally, can have any good thing in their nature, as belonging to it." And Prop. vi., § 17: "Man is wholly unable of himself to work with the grace, neither can he move one step out of the natural condition until the grace lay hold upon him." These passages are typical of many more. It was chiefly when the Friends were trying to be orthodox and logical, that they fell into trouble about "nature." Barclay, who was nothing if not logical, argues desperately that when Paul wrote "the Gentiles do *by nature* the things of the law" (Rom. ii. 14), he meant the opposite of man's real and proper nature, viz., "the spiritual nature which proceedeth from the seed of God in man" ("Apology," Prop. iv. 2). William Penn, after urging repeatedly that the Light Within is "in man but not

The Weakness of Quakerism

"natural" order of the world excluded God; nature itself had been spoiled by the Fall, and remained a world of darkness, subject to the dominion of Satan.

What, then, of their doctrine of the Light Within? It was, as we have seen, the very basis on which they built, and their lives were proof of its reality as an experience; but, when they tried to set it forth in theological language, they failed for want of a true philosophy. They made it something wholly alien to man's nature; a Divine light, supernaturally placed in the dark human creature, like a candle in a lantern;[1] placed there for a season only, and withdrawn if ignored or rejected.[2] It was not an attribute of man, but a "substance" entirely separate from man's own being; it was "a medicine," not a condition of health.[3] "The light of which we speak," says Barclay, "is not only distinct, but of a different nature, from the soul of man and its faculties." Reason may rule men in "things natural," but only this Divine light can rule men in "things spiritual." It is not to be identified with the Conscience, which is a natural gift, any more than a candle is the same as the lantern that holds it.

By thus finding for every man a chance of salvation, even if a brief one, Barclay fancied that he escaped the horrors of the Calvinistic theology, and "justified

---

of man," admits, at last, that it is *natural* to man to have a *supernatural* Light. ("Primitive Christianity Revived," iii., §§ 1, 2, 1696.) The dualism is on the verge of breaking down. If the Friends had pondered on the implications of our Lord's parable of the Sower, where the "seed" is identified with the hearts that receive it, their dualism might have been abandoned altogether (see p. 99).

[1] Barclay, Prop. vi., § 16.
[2] *Ibid.*, § 12.
[3] *Ibid.*, § 14.

Authority and the Light Within

the ways of God to men." His position is certainly a step in advance, for the Calvinist found for the majority of men no chance at all. But it never seems to have occurred to Barclay to ask whether, if the great majority in fact reject the light, ignoring the "day of their visitation," and are consequently plunged into eternal and irretrievable perdition, the world is not a ghastly and hideous failure, and had better not have been created. And, in truth, the Calvinism of Barclay the Scotchman lay only a little way below the surface. Man, he says, can do absolutely nothing to bring about his own salvation; God must have all the glory. The only thing that man can do is to *wait* for the grace to come—for the moving of the Spirit, the shining of the Light—and *not resist* it when it works.[1]

But this "waiting," this "not resisting," is preeminently a work of *faith*. Man's "nature" is, according to Barclay, to resist and not to wait; the faith that can conquer nature is a supernatural gift, equally with the Light itself. "Faith," says Isaac Penington, "is not found in man's nature, so that it is a gift to be waited for and obtained from God." It follows, then, that man can do really nothing; God is wholly responsible for man's destiny; the formulated theology of the early Friends turns out to be, unconsciously but thoroughly, Calvinistic.

[1] Barclay, Prop. v., § 18. Some, he says, there are, "in whom grace so prevaileth that they necessarily obtain salvation, *neither doth God suffer them to resist*. For it were absurd to say that God hath not far otherwise extended himself towards the virgin Mary and the Apostle Paul than towards many others; neither can we affirm that God equally loved the beloved disciple John and Judas the traitor."

The Weakness of Quakerism

Such is, indeed, the inevitable outcome of the dualism with which they started. That dualism made a *real* Divine immanence impossible. God visited the world, but He did not permeate it. God and man were wholly out of organic relation with one another. Since they had nothing in common, the Light must be one of two mutually exclusive things—human or divine. Either it was wholly supernatural and non-human, or else a mere "light of nature" by which man could save himself without Divine intervention. The Quakers recoiled in horror from the latter view, and found themselves shut up in the former, with all its consequences.

The consequences were serious. (1) In the first place, the Quakers had no real answer to the charge, constantly levelled at them, that they made the individual infallible. The Light Within, as they conceived it, left no place for Authority.[1] The individual could be taken possession of by the Divine Spirit and used as an oracular medium, his human faculties wholly in abeyance—just as they, in common with other Christians of that day, imagined the Biblical writers to have been. The Puritans supposed that such infallible inspiration ceased with the completion of the Scriptures; the Quakers extended it to the present

---

[1] Nominally, of course, the Friends recognised the Authority of the Scriptures (see Chapter IV., pp. 39, 40), though they never regarded it as primary; but it was want of clear thought that left them with two concurrent infallibilities, that of the Bible and that of the individual interpreter. They never faced the possibility of two infallible people interpreting differently the teaching of Scripture. That this is no imaginary objection, everyone who has tried to extract a rule of conduct from the recorded sayings of Jesus is, of course, perfectly aware.

Authority and the Light Within

day. Anyone to-day, they imagined, might be a Divine oracle, uttering words full of Divine infallibility.

There is no doubt that many of the early Friends really imagined themselves to be infallible, though they were always willing to be judged by the Scriptures, which they regarded as also infallible. "In the light I meet with infallibility," says Isaac Penington; "The light of God's spirit is a certain and infallible rule, *and the eye that sees it is a certain eye.*"[1] This was their theory, which was obviously fraught with the utmost danger, especially to men like James Nayler, who were naturally prone to extravagance. It is only fair to recognise that in practice, taught by such lapses as that of Nayler, they allowed that "the treasure is in earthen vessels," and that the assertion of personal inspiration must be tempered and tested by the collective inspiration of the Church. The institution of "Elders," in the middle of the eighteenth century, to control the exercise of public ministry, was a practical avowal that the theory, as it had been stated, did not hold good. It meant that, in claiming personal infallibility, the principle of Authority had been overlooked, and that steps were needed to find a place for it.[2]

(2) The idea of a Light wholly supernatural and

---

[1] Quoted by R. M. Jones, "Social Law in the Spiritual World," p. 179.
[2] It may perhaps be thought that an undue space has been devoted to this criticism, since few Quakers to-day would dream of claiming to be infallible. Our reason is that the best grounded objection to the doctrine of the Light Within, as this has been usually stated, has hardly ever yet been admitted or answered. If it is to be adequately met, its force must be admitted, and a better statement sought for.

The Weakness of Quakerism

non-human involved the depreciation of human faculties. In Divine worship the ideal became *cessation of thought*, in order that the Spirit might come in and take possession. This brought forward, in public ministry, persons of a certain psychical temperament—whose sub-conscious life, lying near the surface, was readily brought into play—and kept in the background those who, little subject to these mysterious movements, were more accustomed to the conscious use of their minds. Hence the ministry tended to become rhapsodical; and, while not infrequently it searched in a wonderful manner the hidden depths of the hearers' hearts, it appealed but little to their minds. Sometimes the supernatural character of the Light was so much exalted that every exercise of reason or judgment seemed an obstacle that must at all costs be cleared out of the way. Hence arose a fear of the use of reason in relation to " Divine things " which is a chief secret of the mental poverty that soon overtook the Society of Friends. Since Barclay, it has produced not one profound thinker. The idea became prevalent that all that was needed, in the way of religious teaching, would be supernaturally provided; and the third and fourth generations of Friends were left, to a very large extent, to grow up in ignorance. It was this ignorance that Samuel Fothergill set out to combat by founding Ackworth School, and Joseph John Gurney, two generations later, by instituting Bible teaching. It is this that explains, more than any other cause, the extreme narrowness of outlook that marked many

Authority and the Light Within

of the Friends of the later eighteenth and early nineteenth centuries—the devotion to minutiæ of speech and dress, the fear of any thoughts that did not run upon traditional lines, the desire to cut off everything from the Society that, in act or expression, was not of the perfect pattern.

The early Quakers failed, then, to see through some of the fallacies that were universal in the religious thought of their day, and hence were unable to find a true way of expressing the new truth they had discovered. It is probable that this is one great cause of their failure, after the first generation had passed away, to move the religious world. While it is true that many of their thoughts are now held by spiritually-minded people in all the Churches, this can hardly be put to their credit, as though it were mainly due to missionary toil of theirs. The Friends have been known as quietists and philanthropists, but to the vast majority of people their spiritual ideals and experiences have been almost completely unknown.

It was not to be expected that the Friends should spiritualise the world with a religion that held cheap the mind of man. Nevertheless, such modest achievement as has been won, in the face of the difficulties caused by the absence of a sound basis in thought, is the best tribute to the truth and vitality of their original discovery.

The Society of Friends could hardly have survived at all were it not that it had found a truth which the world needed; and surely the need to-day is as great

The Weakness of Quakerism

as ever. The interest in the "New Theology" shows how men and women are longing for someone who can "speak to their condition." What might the Society of Friends accomplish for the saving of men from unbelief and sin, if only it could, in life as well as words, proclaim worthily the truth for which it stands, and find, in the best philosophic thought and knowledge of the present day, a place for the presence of the Light Within?

X

THE LIGHT WITHIN AND REASON

WE dealt in the last chapter with the mistakes made by the Early Friends, through the limitations of seventeenth-century philosophy, in attempting rigidly to separate God from Nature and the Light Within from human Reason. Essentially their discovery of the Divine immanence linked them on to the mystics of all the Christian ages—to Clement of Alexandria, and, behind him, to Paul and John; but they tried in vain to express this immanence in terms of the Augustinian dualism which had moulded the religious thinking of the western world. So long as God and man were placed in separate chambers of thought, the Light was necessarily either wholly human or wholly Divine. To make it human meant denial of the need for both revelation and salvation; hence it was claimed as absolutely Divine. But this involved the infallibility of each person to whom the Light was given, and the ousting of human faculties from any place in dealing with the things of God. Man had no religious faculty requiring cultivation; religious instruction was needless; the more his mind was emptied—the more it became "like a sheet of blank paper"—the cleaner would it be for the writing upon it of Divine oracles.

Such was the logical outcome of the position to

The Light Within and Reason

which the Friends were driven; and, though they often (like many more) rose superior to their own logic, there remained an inherent weakness which has constantly hindered the delivery of their message. One great need of the present day would seem to be a restatement of the principle of the Light Within, in terms of modern thought and knowledge. For such a statement the writer's ability, and the space afforded by the present work, are alike inadequate; we can only indicate in the broadest manner the lines along which it might well proceed. In endeavouring to lay a philosophic basis for trust in the Inward Light, we must not be understood as making an appeal from revelation to philosophy, as if to something more certain than itself. What we are rather doing is to show that the private and individual certitude, which comes to us through the Light Within but which we cannot communicate, is not weakened but is fortified by the conclusions of a Reason which is common to all thinking people.

While there are many philosophies, there is a general convergence at the present time, among all competent thinkers, in the direction of Idealism. Materialism, as an explanation of the Universe, is out of court to-day; the fallacy has become obvious that would make thought a mere product of material changes. For Thought is the *prius* of all knowledge of matter and force; nothing is known at all except as related to Consciousness; the Mind that perceives relations among objects can be no mere product of the things related, nor can a stream of sensations

Authority and the Light Within

organise experience into a unity.[1] We have experience; our experience is not in detached or unrelated fragments, but forms itself into a cosmos or unity; and this can only mean that what lies at the root of it is not matter but Mind or Reason. So far there is general agreement; and many will go further and agree that the unity of *human*, as distinct from *individual*, experience, implies a Universal Consciousness, of which that of the individual is but (as it were) a focus-point or partial manifestation.

If there were only individual consciousnesses, there might be as many *truths* as there are persons. The fact that we recognise only *one truth*, and all the rest as error, points surely to One Consciousness as that for which the real world exists. Thus, as has been said above, "God is the deepest foundation of all truth, the reality of which phenomena are but appearances, the basis of the distinction we make between truth and falsehood."[2] The world is real; but it has its reality in God, and God alone.

The modern or Idealist philosophy is thus unable to think of either Nature or Man as having any real existence apart from God. Human consciousness, or human personality, is a point at which the Universal Consciousness, or Divine Personality, is manifesting itself. In Biblical language, man was made in the image of God. Reason, therefore, which in the widest sense of the term is identical with Thought or self-consciousness, is in a real sense not only human but

[1] See T. H. Green, "Prolegomena to Ethics," passim.
[2] Chapter VII., p. 68. See also Rufus M. Jones, "Social Law in the Spiritual World," pp. 238-245.

The Light Within and Reason

Divine.[1] In Johannine phraseology, the Divine Logos or Reason was from the beginning with God and was God, and was also the Light of man.

But the word "Reason" is often used, in a narrower sense, to name that particular activity of the mind by which we reach truth *through inference;* as when we say "the roofs are wet, *therefore* it must be raining." And just in so far as "Reason" stands for the process of deliberate reasoning, it is quite rightly distinguished from the "Light Within" (though in truth no part of our mental activity can really dispense with the Light).[2] For there are vast tracts of knowledge, and these among the most important, which cannot be made objects either of direct observation or of cogent inference and demonstration. Nearly all our knowledge of *persons* is of this quality, being based in the last resort on our knowledge of our own consciousness; and so is our knowledge of God and of life in relation to Him. It is in these regions, as we have endeavoured to show in a previous chapter, that the "Light Within" comes most directly into play.[3]

The truth is that *persons* are known to us by the response of our whole personality to theirs; and it is the same with the knowledge of God.[4] We know God

---

[1] T. H. Green, "Works," Vol. III., p. 267.
[2] See Chapter XI., pp. 101—103.
[3] Chapter VII., pp. 66—69.
[4] See Inge, "Personal Idealism and Mysticism," pp. 3 and ff. "There is no separate organ for the apprehension of divine truth, independent of will, feeling, and thought. Our knowledge of God comes to us in the interplay of those faculties." And he quotes the mediæval mystic, Juliana of Norwich, as saying, in words that strike a truer note than Barclay's:—"Our faith cometh of the natural love of the soul, and of the clear light of our reason, and of the steadfast mind, which we have of God in our first making."

Authority and the Light Within

because we are essentially sons; and the sonship within us rises up to meet the Father.[1] Truth is reached in these realms by a kind of intuition, in which true conclusions are arrived at without going through the painful steps of deliberate reasoning. There is here a kind of instinctive and implicit reasoning, which may later on be justified by conscious demonstration; certainly the process is a part of the work of "Reason" in the wide sense of that term. And this inward assurance of truth is, as we have seen, the human side of "the Light Within."

The Light Within may thus be called, under one aspect, a human faculty, if we remember that there is no such thing in our nature as a *separable* faculty, but that always our personality acts as a whole, though in many ways. It is a faculty identical with that whose working we call *faith*. "Faith," says the author of *Hebrews*, in words that summarise what has been said above, "is the reality of things hoped for, the proving of things not seen." It is the power by which we have assurance of things we cannot demonstrate by reasoning. It is the same power that Paul postulates in writing to the Corinthians (though he reserves the word "faith" for a more special use), when he says that the Spirit of God reveals to the "spiritual" man things that the "animal" man cannot receive —that is to say, things that "eye saw not and ear heard not, and that entered not into human understanding."[2]

[1] "Lux Mundi," pp. 15-19.
[2] 1 Cor. ii. 14, 9, 10. The whole of Chapter I. of "Lux Mundi," on "Faith," may well be read in this connection. See also Sermon on Faith in T. H. Green's "Works," as above.

The Light Within and Reason

"The Light Within" is just as much a human faculty as is "Reason" in its widest sense; it is the power of a self-conscious person to enter into communion with God. It is also Divine; for it is God revealing Himself within us. In the depth of every person the Divine and the human meet; as Dr. Rufus Jones has said, "our souls open inwardly into God."

And yet, if this be so, what are we to make of *Sin*, and how can sin separate us from God? The question is closely akin to this other: what is Error, and how can we think thoughts that are not the thoughts of God?

We are bound to recognise, if we are true to the facts of life, without us and within, that there is this disturbing "other," which upsets our fairest philosophies and roughens our smoothest theories. Our life is not, in fact, what we instinctively perceive it was meant to be, what indeed it *is* in essence and in ideal. It is in the language of poetry rather than of strict logic that we can best do justice to the facts we find. Says Augustine:—

> Too late I loved thee, O beauty of ancient days, yet ever new; and lo! thou wert within, and I searching for thee abroad. *Thou wert with me, but I was not with thee.*

And Whittier, expanding this thought:—

> O Love Divine, whose constant beam
> Shines on the eyes that will not see,
> And waits to bless us, while we dream
> Thou leavest us, because we turn from thee.[1]

However we may attempt to explain it, we know that each one of us has the power, and has used it, to

[1] Whittier, "The Shadow and the Light," and note.

Authority and the Light Within

turn from God in thought, which is error, and in will, which is sin. The self, which each one of us is, has aimed at a false independence, has tried to go its own way, has lost the touch and the sight of the God who is ever near. The Light within us has grown dim; darkness has obscured our vision. Yet, dim as it may be, the light is ever there. What can restore its brightness? Nothing but being brought back into the Whole that we have tried to leave; the surrender of our private imaginings to the facts, that we may know the truth; the submission of our private wills to God's Will, that we may do the right.

In every self-conscious life two forces are revealed, good and evil, truth and error, God and what is against God. And life's progress consists in the successful warfare of the one with the other, in the victory of the higher over the lower, in the rule of the higher, which is God within.

In One conscious Life the victory from the first was perfect; and here was shown forth in undimmed splendour, so far as man needed to know it, what God is and what he too may be. Here was the Logos made flesh; the Eternal Light, that lighteth every man, manifested under conditions of space and time. And it is in a vital relation to that Life—not by the acceptance of dogmatic creeds but by the opening of the heart and the surrender of the will—that in all the Christian ages men have known their spiritual vision cleared.

> I say, the acknowledgment of God in Christ,
> Accepted by thy reason, solves for thee
> All questions in the earth and out of it:

The Light Within and Reason

All questions, that is, which need to be answered if we are to become the best that we were meant to be. Some of these questions we will further consider in the following chapters.

XI

THE LIGHT WITHIN AND REASON
(Continued)

WE endeavoured to show, in the last chapter, that a real foundation for the doctrine of the Divine Immanence, and therefore of the Light Within, is afforded by the Idealist Philosophy—which, starting from the unity of human experience, explains that this unity has its basis in the Universal Consciousness whom we call God. Philosophy thus brings God and man very near together; each particular human soul is, in essence and ideal, a partial manifestation of an infinite and eternal Consciousness, apart from whom it would have no real existence. The Light Within, or Reason in its widest sense, is thus seen to be both Divine and human—a faculty of man, which is also the organ of God's communion with him.

Yet, as we saw, this thought of the Divine Immanence in man does not, by itself, adequately cover the facts. It does not explain how the thoughts of man can be other than thoughts of God; that is to say, it renders no clear account of the disturbing elements we call Sin and Error. Nor does it, with indubitable certainty, conserve man's personality—for his sense of individuality might conceivably be an illusion, to be outgrown as he becomes absorbed into the Universal Mind.

The Light Within and Reason

Idealism, if not watched, tends to merge into Pantheism. In other words, the doctrine of the Divine Immanence needs to be balanced with the thought of Divine Transcendence. This Transcendence, if it has never yet found adequate philosophical expression, is none the less amply guaranteed by the religious experience of the human race. Man is not simply of one piece with God. Discord and division have come in; man has, so far at least as his own consciousness is concerned, separated himself from the Divine harmony. Aiming at an independent life, he has lost his true relation, and can only regain it by surrendering himself to the whole. This surrender implies no loss or absorption of personality. It is not that he won his individuality through sin, and will lose it by surrendering himself to God. Sin's *promise*, indeed, is always a higher individuality: "Ye shall be as gods." But the promise is never fulfilled. It is religion's paradox—deepest of truths, but hitherto imperfectly explained by philosophy—that in seeking his own individuality man loses it, while in losing his personality for God's sake he finds it.

Owing, then, to the presence of Sin, the Divine Light does not shine undimmed in the soul of man as he is. Only in One human Life was the will of man so completely one with God's will that the Light was never clouded. Men have sought an unknown God. He has been far beyond and high above any conception they were able to form of Him, any conscious experience possessed by them. They have mistaken anthropomorphic pictures for real existence,

Authority and the Light Within

and fancied that verbal formulæ could do duty for the living God. Nothing but purity of heart has brought them eyes to see; only by doing the will of the Father have they learnt to know. The Divine Transcendence imposes this moral struggle, as a condition of knowing truly the Divine Immanence.

> The toppling crags of duty scaled
> Are close upon the shining table-lands,
> Whereof our God Himself is moon and sun.

It is the Divine Transcendence that is able to give to the Immanence its value and its power. He who is revealed within us is no other than the Infinite, the Unapproachable.

Even for the perfect Life the Divine Transcendence held. "My Father is greater than I." "I can of mine own self do nothing." "I came not to do mine own will." These are characteristic utterances from the Gospel where, in the doctrine of the Logos, the Divine Immanence is most clearly taught. It is not, therefore, human sin alone that compels us to recognise the Divine Transcendence; the One perfect human Life felt itself, *as human*, far short of the absolute Divine infinitude.[1]

Has the effect of Sin been to darken man's mind

---

[1] But is not Jesus reported as saying (John x. 30), "I and the Father are one?" Yes; but unless we are to attribute to Him a double consciousness, of which there is not one trace on the pages of the Gospels, we are bound, in the light of those other passages quoted, to interpret the "oneness" here spoken of as *oneness of will and purpose*, not of absolute consciousness. This agrees with the verses that precede and follow. The sheep that belong to Jesus belong equally to the Father, because the Father and the Son are one in spirit. "Say ye, thou blasphemest, because I said I am *the Son* of God?" It is ethical, not metaphysical, oneness that is here claimed.

The Light Within and Reason

completely, and utterly to disable his Reason from finding its way to truth and to God? "Yes," has been the "orthodox" answer, and, as we saw, the early Quakers adopted it without question. But *it is not true*. The doctrine of total human depravity had its sole foundation in a literal interpretation of certain texts of Scripture; it is contradicted by all our experience of life, and also by the plain teaching of the Master Himself. He appeals to the good human qualities even of those who are "evil" (Matt. vii. 11), and marks a difference between good men and evil men (Matt. xii. 35). He appeals to an inward witness even in His opponents, that what He says is true (John viii. 46; Luke xii. 57). In His parable of the Sower (Mark iv. 3-20) the seed that is sown is identified with the hearts that receive it: it is *they* that are "sown" by the way side, upon the rocky places, among the thorns, and upon the good ground. In view of His oft-repeated words about children (Mark x. 13-16, etc.), how can anyone dare to say that children, till baptized or converted, are wholly evil and "under the wrath of God?" We cannot possibly admit that man, as man, is hopelessly corrupt and dark.

Nor can we allow, with Barclay, that while human Reason is in its right sphere in dealing with "things natural," it has no power to meddle with "things spiritual."[1] For there is no real dividing line between the two—the dualism which Barclay took for granted having broken down. *All* our experience is ours only as we are spiritual, that is to say self-conscious, beings.

---

[1] Barclay, "Apology," Prop. vi., § 16.

Authority and the Light Within

Where, for instance, does ethics come—the discussion of what is right and what is wrong in conduct? It is only for spiritual beings that the words right and wrong have any meaning; yet there is always need for the criticism, by Reason, of the conventional standards that society sets up, and none have practised this criticism more than the Quakers. It was enlightened Reason that John Woolman followed, when he tested the practices of his contemporaries, in such things as slave-holding, land renting and luxurious living, by "the spirit of pure wisdom." "He that is spiritual," says Paul (1 Cor. ii. 15) "examineth all things." It is not said that he must not examine things that are spiritual.

There is, indeed, a possible misuse of Reason which must be allowed for, and which is *not* following "the spirit of pure wisdom." It is possible for the individual, or for a section of humanity, to insist that that alone is "reasonable" which promotes its interests, regardless of the wider interests of humanity and the race. "Why should I consider posterity? What has posterity done for me?" The questions, for example, of population, and of the alleged failure of marriage to promote happiness, are often argued as if the interests of two, or a few, human beings were alone concerned; whereas it is clear that the way these questions are answered may vitally affect the race. Such selfish short-sightedness was assumed by Benjamin Kidd, in his "Social Evolution," to be the normal quality of Reason; but this is surely a grave mistake. *True* Reason, in its widest sense, is the

The Light Within and Reason

Universal Consciousness within us; it is God thinking His thoughts in man. The individual is brought down and humbled as he follows it—as he strives, that is, to yield up his opinions to truth, his theories to facts, his private interest to the public good, his mind to the mind of God.

There is no opposition between true Reason and the Faith which receives and uses the Light Within.

But objection may be taken on another ground, if Reason is taken in the more limited sense of Reasoning.[1] It may be urged, with much force, that there is in religious truth an infinite or expansive element, such as cannot be confined within the precise and definite categories of thought with which alone the reasoning intellect can properly deal. There is, to-day, in many minds, an impatience with theological dogma, which is largely healthy—a feeling that religious thoughts are spoiled and vulgarised by being subjected to processes of rigid analysis and definition. We cannot set down in a catalogue the beauties of the dawn; why should we think of defining and systematising the "attributes of God," or the meaning of Christ's person and work? Why should we refuse to entertain such ideas, until we can make them the objects of rounded and finished demonstration?

There is much truth in this view; but it does not follow that Reason, even in that limited sense, has not a rightful and necessary part to play in relation to religious truth. We may readily allow that it is a

[1] See Chapter X., p. 91.

Authority and the Light Within

lower gift than the Light Within and the Faith that receives this light. But it is not the plan on which God's universe is built, that the higher principle should maintain itself by ruling out the lower; rather must it absorb and transform it. Life maintains itself by taking up and vivifying inorganic matter; the spirit lives in man by making the bodily powers its organs. So Faith may well make use of Reason, accepting, enlightening, clarifying it. Even Barclay, in a noteworthy passage, recognises this:—

> Even as the moon borrows her light from the sun, so ought men, if they would be rightly and comfortably ordered in natural things, to have their reason enlightened by this divine and pure light. Which enlightened reason, in those that obey and follow this true light, we confess may be useful to man even in spiritual things, as it is still subservient and subject to the other; even as the animal life in man, regulated and ordered by his reason, helps him in going about things that are rational.[2]

There is much for Reason to do, in the spiritual sphere, which is quite indispensable. In the first place, the Light Within yields an assurance of truth which, though priceless, and necessary for our highest life, is yet personal and incommunicable. You can only assure a person who cannot see what you see, that, if he will become as you are, he will see it. The assertion may well appear dogmatic, and be unconvincing. Reason, on the other hand, is *collective*, and not merely individual. What is once *proved true* is true for all who know the facts, and takes its place as a part of the recognised order of the world.

Secondly, enlightened Reason may be just as

[2] "Apology," Prop. vi., § 16.

The Light Within and Reason

usefully employed in ordering the material of religious knowledge as in constructing theories in other departments of study. It is true that the theory of sound will never make a musician, yet a musician may be the better for a knowledge of the theory.

> In like manner, religion exists and must exist as a life and experience, before it can be made the object of reflective thought; but there is no more reason in this than in other instances, why experimental knowledge should exclude scientific knowledge.[1]

Such reasoned and "scientific knowledge" is what constitutes a sound Theology.

Again, there is much for Reason to do in purifying the affirmations of Faith from the false elements that too easily enter into them: such as the confusion between the conventional framework of ideas, within which Faith is accustomed to move, and that inner kernel which is really its object. A Roman Catholic, for example, may have the same inward assurance of the help of the Virgin or the Saints, that he has of Divine answer to his prayer. Yet we are sure that, while the latter is of the kernel, the former is merely of the "framework." And we have already seen how necessary it is, for a satisfying statement of Christian truth, that we should transcend the dualism of natural and supernatural which hampered the thinking of the seventeenth century. Such a separation of false elements from true, which is needed right through the range of Christian beliefs, is only to be accomplished by the diligent use of the enlightened Reason.

[1] John Caird, "Fundamental Ideas of Christianity," Vol. I. p. 42. (The whole of this chapter, "Faith and Reason," may well be read.)

XII

THE LIGHT WITHIN AND CONSCIENCE

THE attempt has sometimes been made, by loose thinkers, to smooth away some of the difficulties that necessarily attend the exposition of the Light Within, by identifying it with the Conscience. The result of such identification is unfortunate. The way is open for the unanswerable objection, If Conscience is indeed the Voice of God in man, why does it say one thing to one man and another to another? Why does it tell a Moslem that polygamy is right and the drinking of alcohol wrong, while it tells Christians that polygamy is wrong, and convinces many of them that moderate drinking is right? Why does it divide Christians into hostile camps on such questions as War and Slavery—allowing many Christians still to support War, just as, a century ago, learned divines wrote volumes to prove Slavery a Divine institution? The result of such objections is to discredit the reality of any faculty in man whereby God comes into immediate communication with him.

Plainly we need a clearer understanding of what is meant both by the Light Within and by Conscience. In Chapter VII., pp. 65—69, we endeavoured to set forth the different conceptions covered by the phrase "The Light Within," as follows :—

(*a*) A personal and individual apprehension of truth,

The Light Within and Conscience

as distinguished from a belief resting on the authority of others.

(*b*) A perception of *moral* truth: *i.e.*, the power to distinguish right from wrong, with the consciousness that we "ought" to pursue the one and avoid the other.

(*c*) The sense of individual duty in particulars: the consciousness of a "call" or "mission."

(*d*) The power by which we learn "Divine Truth": *i.e.*, truth as to the being and character of God, and of life in relation to Him.

It will be seen at once that the application of the term "The Light Within" is wider than that which is given to the word "Conscience." The latter term may be said to be equivalent to the second only of the above four headings. It is possible that some persons might employ it also for the third, saying it is their "Conscience" that directs them into a particular course of action; but as a rule the function of Conscience is held to be to lay upon men, not their individual obligations, but the moral duties that are common to them with others.

And even here an important distinction arises, as to the use of the word Conscience. Dr. Martineau and others have insisted on the difference between the power to distinguish right and wrong (with the sense of "ought" that accompanies it), and the judgment that, in a particular moral question, one class of conduct is right and another wrong. It is one thing to be so constituted as to be compelled to distinguish between higher and lower; it is another to say, in any

Authority and the Light Within

particular problem, *this* is the higher, *that* the lower. Christians, Turks, and all self-conscious beings are alike in possessing, more or less highly developed, some sense of right and wrong. The lowest savage knows that he "ought" to observe the tribal customs. But, possessing in common the faculty that compels them to moral distinctions, men differ enormously in the use they make of it.

It is only in the first, or broader, sense of the term Conscience, that it can be identified with the Light Within. We can say that it is because we have a Divine Light within the soul that we all, as human beings, know that there is a *right* which we ought to follow; we cannot say that it is the Light Within that directly sets up our conventional moral standards. For, as we have seen, these depend upon circumstances, changing from one age to another, and varying with education and environment.

The early Quakers were right in distinguishing the Light Within from this empirical Conscience; but they did not succeed in formulating the distinction satisfactorily. The "candle in the lantern" simile did not carry them very far. Barclay quite dogmatically states[1] that the Light of Christ in a Moslem, if properly attended to, would inform him not only that it is wrong to have more than one wife, but that Mohammed was an impostor. He seems to have been writing from theory rather than from experience; being, of course, compelled to infer, on his dualistic basis, that, if the Light was in every man, and if

[1] "Apology," Prop. vi., § 16.

The Light Within and Conscience

it was Divine and not human, then every man possessed (if he would use it) an infallible knowledge of right and wrong. That this theory is contradicted by experience is, we believe, one great reason why the doctrine of the Light Within was, for many minds, discredited.

Not without importance, then, is the search for a true distinction; and it is, we believe, along the lines indicated by Martineau that we shall find it. By "Conscience," in the empirical or narrower sense, we understand the judgment which, in a particular issue, pronounces one class of conduct right and another wrong. This, as we have seen, results from training and environment; it is historically conditioned. The "Light Within," on the other hand, is the outcome of that Divine element in man, that spark of the Universal Consciousness, which makes him a self-determining agent, and not a mere creature of impulse. It enables him to hold before his mind different ideals, or courses of conduct; to picture himself as finding satisfaction in one or another; and to decide which shall be the one with which he chooses to identify himself. It forces upon him the conviction that these ideal courses are often of different moral worth, as higher or lower; and that he "ought" to choose that which appears to him the highest.

It is the presence of this Divine faculty in man that has produced the Conscience, and has been the cause of its gradual illumination, as man has risen from barbarism to comparative civilisation. It is because he

Authority and the Light Within

has been capable of ideals, that one ideal after another, in ascending series, has drawn him upward. The Conscience, at any particular stage of moral evolution, was conditioned by custom, by law, by tradition; but there was always something behind it, capable of responding to a higher ideal when presented.

To take but a single instance. To Greek and Jew, alike, the thought of a universal Brotherhood, if it occurred at all, was mere fanatical foolishness. The Greek felt the tie of duty to fellow-Greeks, but little, if at all, to barbarians, slaves, or women. The Jew thought himself right in hating Samaritans and Gentiles. Some of his teachers, in the days of the Apostles, were instructing him that kind actions done to aliens were wrong. But a few Roman Stoics and jurists had discerned, even before the Christian Era, that mankind is bound together by ties that go deeper than race or nation [1]; and this, which remained with them a poetic sentiment that was far from influencing the general mind, was made by Jesus Christ into "current coin." By His teaching and practice He definitely widened the area of "neighbour"-hood to cover all mankind; and placed it, for those who accepted Him, on the firm basis of a Divine revelation, making it a necessary consequence of the universal Fatherhood of God.

How was it that His ideal of brotherhood, which struck right across the most ingrained convictions and the most venerable institutions of the ancient

[1] For quotations see Lecky, " History of European Morals," Vol. I., pp. 240, 241.

The Light Within and Conscience

world, was able to shatter these and establish itself upon their ruins? Only because there was something of God in men which enabled them to discern its truth; which forced them to recognise that, being higher than their old ideals, it must be followed; which gradually formed in them a new Conscience. This new conscience is far from being complete yet. The civilised nations have, indeed, (in theory at least) put an end to slavery, and the exploitation of women for the benefit of men; but war still finds "Christian" defenders; the statesmanship of great nations is based avowedly on undiluted national selfishness; and few as yet are sensitive to the injustice which denies to the great masses of our people, who do for us the hard manual work of life, any share in that heritage of culture and refined enjoyment without which, to us who have it, life would be almost worthless.

Through all stages of moral evolution, from first to last, it has been the Light Within that has developed, enlightened, educated, the human Conscience. From the first rude beginnings of human society, it was this that made man conscious, however dimly, that his life was bound up with the lives of others, that his inclinations must be curbed for the common good, that he must not transgress the limits of authoritative custom. It was this that, from time to time, burned in the hearts of seers and prophets and leaders of new religions, teaching them new truth, enlarging their ideals, making them willing to suffer for violating, in obedience to a law within, the moral standards of their age; bringing home to their fellows the truth

Authority and the Light Within

and goodness of the new ideals, and so developing a new conscience. It is to this we must look to enlighten our own minds, and the minds of our contemporaries, with a clear vision as to the application, under present conditions, of the universal brotherhood in which, as Christians, we profess to believe. It is this alone that can raise up for us a new John Woolman, and give us receptive ears to hear his message.

We may be thankful that our Divine Master made no attempt to construct a new Decalogue, crystallising in a formula the moral duties of men. He left the field open for indefinite expansion, and trusted His own living Spirit to afford the necessary enlightenment from age to age. He contented Himself with two commandments—love to God and love to man—which are not so much precepts as an expression of the ultimate moral basis: that life must be lived in a right correspondence with our spiritual environment, both in the unseen and the seen. It is on this basis that every ethical system, in every age, must always rest.[1]

What we have been trying to show is that the variation, from age to age and from land to land, of the moral standard by which men live, is no disproof of the existence of a Divine Light within their souls. The moral standard *must* vary, according to the degree of enlightenment men have reached. Neither any single "duty," nor the nature of the moral good which informs all "duties," is so com-

[1] See "Ecce Homo," chapter on "The Enthusiasm of Humanity."

The Light Within and Conscience

pletely known to us that it can be adequately and finally expressed in any form of words. There is in it something of the infinite—something of the nature of God Himself—so that our knowledge of it is ever growing, never complete.[1] No empirical moral judgment is ever final or exhaustive; and this fact may comfort us in some of our moral perplexities.[2]

Yet we are not thereby in any degree absolved from the necessity of seeking ever for the highest; nor deprived of the happy faith that each surrendered will and obedient heart may know, if the inward eye is ever open to the Light, the priceless blessing of "a conscience void of offence."

[1] See Green, "Prolegomena to Ethics," pp. 178 and ff.
[2] The fact, for example, that it is no easy matter so to define War as to say precisely what use of force constitutes War, is no reason for doubting the dictum of the enlightened Christian conscience, that War is wrong.

XIII

THE LIGHT WITHIN AND ATONEMENT

ONE of the oldest objections to the teaching of the Light Within is that it seems to make the Atonement needless. If all men have the Spirit of God, what becomes of the supposed necessity for Conversion and the New Birth? Is it not mere idle talk?

Such, indeed, might be the logical answer reached on the lines of monistic philosophy, if taken as a complete and satisfying basis for religious faith. But there are no grounds for bringing this charge of minimising the necessity of Atonement against the early Quakers, nor are there (we trust) against the attempt which has been made in these pages to restate in modern form their doctrine of the Light Within.

The Friends took over, as we have seen, from the theology of their day the foundation doctrine of the total depravity of human nature, ruined once for all by the fall of Adam. There could, therefore, be no question in their minds as to the necessity for Atonement. Man was totally unable to save himself; hence, if God had not come to his rescue in the person of Jesus Christ, his case would have been hopeless. The source and root of human salvation they found in the universal love of God, who had

The Light Within and Atonement

sent His Son not merely to rescue men from eternal ruin, but to change their very nature.[1]

The most valuable part of the teaching of the early Quakers in regard to the Atonement was their insistence that it was no mere "transaction," external to ourselves, but that its real meaning and purpose was to be looked for in the change of our personality. Barclay rejects as unscriptural the phrase "imputed righteousness," insisting that to "justify" means to "makes righteous," and that justification is nothing if it is not also sanctification.[2] He notes two elements in the atoning work of Christ: the first is *for* us—in the "purchase" for us of a Divine light, or "seed," which constitutes our "capacity for salvation," and is, indeed (for him) identical with the "Light Within"; the second is *in* us.

> The second is that whereby we witness and know this pure and perfect redemption *in ourselves*, purifying, cleansing and redeeming us from the power of corruption, and bringing us into unity, favour and friendship with God.

In thus insisting on the inward work of Atonement, Barclay was undoubtedly much nearer to the real thoughts of the New Testament than were most of the Puritan theologians of his day;[3] we could wish

---

[1] The early Friends did not free themselves from employing at times the current language about the Sacrifice of Christ removing, or qualifying, the Divine wrath. Barclay uses the popular, but quite unscriptural, phrases that, in virtue of the death and sufferings of Christ, "God is reconciled to us," because "satisfaction has been made to His justice." ("Apology," Prop. vii., § 3, etc.) But these terms do not express, and are not in true harmony with, his real thought.

[2] "Apology," Prop. vii., § 6, 4.

[3] It is extremely important to notice that. in almost every one of the classical "Atonement" passages in the New Testament, the purpose of the death of Christ is declared to be the working of a change *in us*: *e.g.*, 2 Cor. v. 15, 21; Gal. i. 4; Heb. ix. 14; 1 Peter ii. 24; 1 John iv. 9—11, etc.

Authority and the Light Within

that he had been able to follow out his thoughts to their legitimate development. The imperfection of men's knowledge of Personality in the seventeenth century stood in his way; yet he speaks of

> That communication of the goods of Christ unto us, by which we come to be partakers of the Divine nature, and are made one with Him, as the branches with the vine, and have a title and right to what He hath done and suffered for us; so that His obedience becomes ours, His righteousness ours, His death and sufferings ours.

It is probably safe to say that only along the line of thought here indicated—that of the *identification* of Christ with God on the one hand and man on the other, which is the kernel of the theology of Paul[1] and John (little as this has been understood), will the Atonement hold its place in the minds of thinking men. The crude doctrine of "substitution"—which rests on the idea of *separate* personalities, and represents Christ as enduring the wrath of God, suffering instead of us a punishment which had to be inflicted on someone—is untrue to the real meaning of the New Testament, and was not held by most of the early Friends. The "mystics," with one consent, have gone deeper.[2] They have felt out after a thought of "*conjunct*" personality, which the psychological study of our day is rendering more and more intelligible.

In the New Testament, Atonement is Reconciliation—the reconciliation of man to God. Everyone

---

[1] It has been well said that the key to Paul's evangelicalism is to be found in his mysticism. We cannot understand the third chapter of Romans until we have mastered the sixth.

[2] See Moberly, "Atonement and Personality," passim. Also "A Little Book of Heavenly Wisdom," edited by E. C. Gregory, Introduction, p. xxv., and extracts.

The Light Within and Atonement

who faces the facts of life, and whose eyes are open to the tragedy of human things, must recognise that Reconciliation is needed. Discord has come into the life of self-concious beings—discord of a different kind from any that we may think we see in the life of plants and animals—and man is unable to restore the harmony. Ethical treatises may define the nature of the good, but not one can remedy the divided will, or offer a cure for the general malady, "when I would do good, evil is present with me."[1] Social Utopias may be planned with consummate skill, but one and all make shipwreck if they have forgotten to take account of human selfishness.

That is, surely, where Christianity "comes in," with its offer of Atonement or Reconciliation. It is the supreme offer for man's supreme need. How shall the gulf be bridged between man's actual and his ideal, between human sin and Divine holiness? The answer is in the Cross of Christ.

[In Christ] we discover—it is the main miracle of the Gospel—that the original movement to bridge the chasm comes from the Divine side. What man hoped to do, but could not, with his bleating lamb and timid dove, God Himself has done. He has reached across the chasm, taking on Himself the sacrifice and cost, to show the sinner that the only obstruction to peace and reconciliation is in the sinner himself. "This is love, not that we loved Him, but that He loved us," and this is sacrifice, not that we give our bulls and goats to please Him, but that He gives Himself to draw us.[2]

It seems necessary thus to clear the ground for our consideration of the relation between Atonement

---

[1] Compare Lofthouse, "Ethics and Atonement," chapter on "Reconciliation."
[2] Rufus M. Jones, "The Double Search," p. 64.

Authority and the Light Within

and the Light Within, by making clear what we understand by Atonement. If we can hold quite steadily this inward view, which is certainly the main part of the New Testament conception, we shall see that, so far from there being any conflict, they are complementary aspects of the mighty process whereby God is communicating Himself to men.

It is as we are reconciled to God, as He takes possession of us, that our spiritual eyes are opened to behold clearly that of which before we were but dimly conscious.

There is, surely, a permanent value, for helping our thoughts on these difficult matters, in the Johannine conception of the Logos—a view which, whatever may be the date of the Gospel and first Epistle attributed to John (and this can hardly be later than 110 A.D.), is found, it should be remembered, in almost identical substance, though without the use of the formal term "Logos," in many passages of Paul's Epistles (the earliest Christian documents in existence), some of which were written within thirty years of the death of Christ.[1] In the prologue to the fourth Gospel, the Divine Logos is introduced as having always been with man, as "the Light that lighteth every man" (John i. 9); so that all men are in some measure "taught of God," and some of them "hear" and "learn" from Him (vi. 45). In the fulness of time "the Word becomes flesh" (i. 14): the diffused

---

[1] For instance, 1 Cor. viii. 6; Gal. ii. 20; Phil. ii. 6; Col. i. 15, 16, iii. 11; Eph. i. 10, etc. See Inge, "Personal Idealism and Mysticism," pp. 47—55.

The Light Within and Atonement

Light is (so to say) focussed in a perfect human personality, in whom therefore the Father is revealed. Those who have been truly "hearing and learning" from the Father come gladly to this clearer Light as soon as it is made known to them; while those who do evil turn their backs upon it (vi. 45; iii. 20, 21). "In Him is *life*"; and those who "receive" Him receive life and are truly "born anew" (iii. 3): their life being no longer as a mere seed, but springing into leaf and flower, and "bearing fruit" as they "abide" in union with Him (xv. 4). He has, indeed, been "working," with the Father, from the beginning, not only in the world of Nature but in the hearts of men (v. 17); but it is only as manifested in the flesh, and giving up His life for the life of the world (vi. 51), that He can fully accomplish His work of revealing the Father and bringing men to Him.

It is perfectly clear that the writer of this Gospel feels no sort of contradiction between the statements "They shall all be taught of God," and "No man cometh unto the Father but by Me" (xiv. 6). It *was* through the eternal Logos that they had been "taught of God" even before they knew Christ in the flesh; and those who are "of the truth" and have taken heed to the teaching, embrace with joy the fuller revelation as soon as it is given them. It is not that these *can do without* the "new birth" of the Spirit; it is that they are in such an attitude of soul that they receive with open arms the fuller life, and come gladly to the Father whom Christ reveals, whom before they had known but dimly.

Authority and the Light Within

The essential work of Jesus, as presented in this fourth Gospel, is therefore *to communicate life* to men—to bring them out of the death of sin into the life of God. Life is offered to all who will come into a right relation with Himself, when He is made known to them—a relation variously described as "believing," "receiving," "knowing," "hearing," "seeing" Him. The relation to God into which this brings them is identical with that which Paul calls Reconciliation; and *those who thus come to share the sonship of Christ share also, according to their measure, His clearness of spiritual vision.*

We see now the difference between the vague, diffused, germ-like faculty of inward vision possessed by mankind in general, and that which comes with the reception into our souls, not as a creed but as a soul-cleansing experience, of the clear light that shines in the face of Jesus Christ. It is, after all, the pure in heart who see; it is those whose natures are renewed by the Spirit of the Crucified who come into full possession of their powers of spiritual vision.[1] He has, indeed, never been far from any of us. Without our knowing it, He

> Is yet the fountain light of all our day,
> Is yet the master light of all our seeing;

but life is a new thing to us when we can discern that this, which has been but as a vaguely-conceived principle, is no other than the Light of the World which shines in the person of our Lord.

[1] In this sense, Barclay's doctrine of the Light being "purchased" for us, by the death of Christ, seems to be justified. But he meant more than this.

The Light Within and Atonement

That which before was but a dim foreshadowing, a far-off ideal—a better nature which we vainly strove, or else cared not, to realise—has taken visible form, once for all, before our eyes. The life and sacrificial death of Jesus present to us at once the perfect reality of our own true nature, and the very heart of God Himself. He wins us by sharing our sorrow, even unto death, that we may share His life. The promise of His Spirit is the promise that the work is to be effectual, if we will have it so—that He, our better self, shall become our actual self, that we may become "one with Him," that He may be "all, and in all."

And so the Light Within and the Atonement are names we give to two complementary aspects of that mighty process whereby God communicates Himself to man that man may become one with God.

XIV

THE LIGHT WITHIN AND THE HOLY SPIRIT

Is the Light Within identical with the Holy Spirit? If so, in what sense is Christianity pre-eminently "the religion of the Spirit"? If all men have within them the Spirit of God, why should we think it needful to try to win them to Jesus Christ? Does not the teaching of the Inward Light cut away the reason and the motive of all Christian missions whatever, unless as purely educative and civilising agencies? What reality, on this basis, can we attach to such terms as Sin, Redemption, and the Baptism of the Spirit?

It is such thoughts as these that, as we noticed in the last chapter, have led many (some, even, in later days, in the Society of Friends itself) to reject as un-Christian the teaching of the Light Within. And yet it is obvious, to all who know the facts, that no Christians have ever held more firmly or more unitedly to this teaching than the Early Quakers, and that none were more fervent Christian missionaries. And it requires but little study of their lives and writings to convince every candid student that their missionary zeal and success was not in spite of, but because of, their strong conviction that in every man there was something that could respond to their

The Light Within and the Holy Spirit

message—an "inward witness" that would, if listened to, bring home its soul-cleansing truth.[1]

In the last chapter it was shown how, in the Johannine theology, two apparently conflicting thoughts were reconciled: of a Light that has always and everywhere been the Light of men, and of the one true Light that has shone, once for all, in the face of Jesus Christ. The doctrine of the Logos brought the two together, and bound them into indissoluble union. The doctrine of the Spirit, which fills the *Acts* and most of the Epistles, is its natural complement. The Light of men, which in the Incarnation had been focussed for a brief season in a perfect human life, had now returned into the unseen, but was with men just as truly and unmistakably as when Jesus was here on earth. Speaking of the days of His flesh, "The Spirit was not yet," says the fourth Evangelist, "because Jesus was not yet glorified" (John vii. 39). He cannot really mean that the resurrection of the Lord made a change in the Divine nature. His words are, surely, a strong and startling assertion of the new *apprehension* of God and of His presence that was now possible for men. So new, so full, so clear and satisfying, was the manifestation of God in

[1] "There is a little thread of divinest melody running through the poor heart of man. Christ takes these threads of melody into His own most perfect life, and shows what the music of humanity is; and, looking at Christ in His perfection, we look through Christ to man in his deepest degradation, and we see that the man lowest in the mire has th- thread of melody in his heart, which may become a great music in Christ. It is there, waiting to be discovered; and we must remember the dignity of human nature if we are to begin to feel about men as Christ felt." (W. J. Dawson, "The Evangelistic Note." Hodder and Stoughton, 1905).

Authority and the Light Within

the Spirit of the risen Lord, compared with anything that men had known of Him before, that it might almost seem as if God Himself had enlarged His own being. And this was not the experience of the few who had been privileged to know Jesus in the flesh. "Of His fulness we all received," says the same writer, "and grace upon grace" (John i. 16): he appeals fearlessly to the witness within his readers (most, if not all, of whom had heard of Christ "by the hearing of faith" alone), that they were, in actual experience, drawing upon an inexhaustible supply of power and love.

In a previous chapter[1] we suggested that it was because the first Christians were so filled with this experience, that they rarely felt the necessity of appealing, for their authority, to words uttered by their Master in the flesh, and never looked back to the days of His outward presence with regret, as to a time when God was nearer to men, and His will more clearly to be known. The early Church, as we there showed, was the Church of *an inspired people*; to be a Christian was essentially to have been baptized with the Spirit of Christ. Jesus by His death had redeemed them from the life of sin, and had brought them, according to their measure, into the same consciousness of sonship with God that He Himself enjoyed. It was this consciousness of a personal relation to God, coupled with a new moral power to live according to His will, and a new experience of "love shed abroad in the heart," which constituted the

[1] Chapter VI., pp. 55—59.

The Light Within and the Holy Spirit

essence of Christianity, and which is spoken of by Paul as "the spirit of adoption, whereby we cry, 'Abba, Father'" (Rom. viii. 15). The Spirit was to be known by its fruit—"love, joy, peace, long-suffering, kindness, self-control" (Gal. v. 22).

It is clear that the speculative question which has troubled some modern minds—whether the Light Within, apart from the Spirit of Christ consciously experienced in the heart, was enough for salvation—would have had little meaning for these early Christians. Salvation meant little or nothing to them as safety for the next world merely—it was a consciousness of having been redeemed from sin here and now. And this experience, quite obviously, was bound up with some knowledge of the historic Christ—with reception of the apostolic message. Whether they ever consciously asked themselves what would be the future of those who died without it is not clear; but Paul at any rate seems to look forward to the time when Christ shall triumph in all hearts, even in those who are now rejecting Him (Rom. xi. 11, 12, 25—27), —just as Jesus in the fourth Gospel anticipates a day when He shall be acknowledged even by His enemies (John viii. 28). The New Testament scarcely gives material for a dogmatic answer, beyond the principle which (as was pointed out in the last chapter) is fundamental in the fourth Gospel: that those who are living in obedience to the light they have will joyfully accept the fuller Light as soon as it is made known to them (John iii. 21; vi. 45). This principle we may surely carry by faith into the world beyond the grave.

Authority and the Light Within

It will be seen that the Holy Spirit, in the New Testament, is always regarded as the source of Christian experience: the time had not come when the Greek intellect, speculating upon the how and the why, and having lost much of the early glow, erected the Spirit into a metaphysical entity. That process may have been inevitable, and it is no part of our present purpose, even had we the knowledge and ability, to discuss questions of abstract theology. It is clear that the true life of Christians in all ages, and most of all in times of spiritual renewal, like the Reformation and the Quaker revival, has not rested upon abstract thought, but upon concrete experience. The attempt to define a Christian as one who, submitting to outward authority, whether of Church or book, professes a certain creed, belongs to days of weakness and not to days of power. When the Spirit is a felt reality, His witness is within.

The doctrine of the Spirit, as it is expressed by Paul and John, is always a thought of God, present in the Spirit of the risen Jesus, and manifesting Himself in the renewed personalities of men. It is not that there is a Power, apart from men, which is added to or supplements some power of right living which they themselves already possess. The beautiful figure of the Paraclete or Helper is a favourite with John, but it does not fully express his thought. Just as, with Paul, the wrestling of the soul after a fuller experience *is* the Spirit "groaning" within it (Rom. viii. 23, 26), so, with John, the new moral life, and the power to love, *are* the Spirit of God

The Light Within and the Holy Spirit

"abiding" in us (1 John iii. 9, 24; iv. 12, 13, etc.). The old self-seeking nature of men is transformed into a new nature which is one with the Spirit of Jesus, and which therefore seeks God and men in love: "If any man be in Christ, there is a new creation; old things are passed away, behold all things are become new" (2 Cor. v. 17); "We are transformed into [His] image from glory to glory, even as by the Lord who is the Spirit" (2 Cor. iii. 18).[1]

We cannot rightly interpret these great thoughts if we suppose that the apostolic writers thought of this mighty transformation as the thrusting into the human soul, by an outside power, of something wholly alien to its true nature. Rather, the new nature *is* the true nature; it is that for which man was created, when "made in the image of God," coming to its own. The "I" which was "crucified with Christ" was a false and usurping self; the true self is the "I" which lives because "Christ liveth in me" (Gal. ii. 20). There has always been that in man which was capable thus of becoming one with Christ, which in this union, when the "body of sin" is "done away," by sharing in His death, becomes, by resurrection with Christ, the man's real self. And so the Holy Spirit is not only God but is also the immanent life of man—is that for which he was created, the flower and fruit of that "Divine seed," or "light within" him, which has always been his

---

[1] See Sabatier, "Religions of Authority," p. 307. "Supernatural gifts become natural; or rather, at this mystical height, the antithesis becomes meaningless and is obliterated."

Authority and the Light Within

better self, the pledge and the promise that he could become one with God.[1]

We need not go up to heaven to bring Christ down from above, or back to a dim and vanished age with painful research, to revive a fading image of the past. He is near us, here and now, the light of all our seeing, the ever present, inexhaustible source and well spring of spiritual life and strength and joy. In the living experience of every Christian spirit, if we but read it truly, there is the witness to the abiding presence of another and higher, raising it ever above itself, the irrefragable proof that that redeeming, hallowing, saving spirit, which for a few brief years identified itself with a perfect human personality, is not a thing of the past, but a living operating spirit and power, imparting to every soul that will but open itself to receive it, the strength, the purity, the peace of a life that is one with the very life of God.[2]

[1] See Moberly, "Atonement and Personality," chapter on "The Holy Spirit."
[2] John Caird, "Fundamental Ideas of Christianity," Vol. II., p. 99.

XV

SUMMARY

IT only remains now to draw together the threads of our discussion of this, which is perhaps the most living and pressing question of our day, and to make clear, if possible, whither it is all tending, and what appears to us the safe path along which the Christian pilgrim may journey, in quietness and assurance, towards the goal of the Kingdom of God.

We started from the position that Authority, in the sense of a larger knowledge than any possessed by the individual, is a necessary consequence of the fact that he is in this world not as an isolated unit, but as a member of a society, having behind him and about him the accumulated treasures of knowledge and experience won by the generations of the past. Every person, who knows more and who can see further than he can, speaks to him with a measure of authority, to which, under ordinary circumstances, he naturally and spontaneously yields assent. Yet such authority is limited and provisional, and can only rightly perform its function by seeking to efface itself and to make way for the autonomy of the individual. It must ever seek to train human souls towards such a personal apprehension of truth and goodness as shall make them strong and (in the true sense) self-reliant. To crush their independence is self-destructive, for it

Authority and the Light Within

is only out of strong and developed individuality that a vigorous society can be constructed.

It is in the realm of spiritual knowledge—of apprehension of those eternal realities that lie in the dim region behind the veil of time and sense—that the craving for final and infallible authority is most keenly felt, and that efforts have been most freely made to provide absolute standards of truth and conduct. Recognising that God is the source of all spiritual authority, and that His authority is indeed final and infallible, we noted that the knowledge of God is inward and not outward, and that, before His authority could be made available, as facts can, to form a common standard, it would have to be mediated to men through something in the outward.

We passed in review the most noteworthy of the efforts to find such a common standard—the claim of the Catholic to have discovered it in an infallible Church, and of the Protestant in an infallible Bible. We were compelled to show, by appeal to reason and history, the hopeless failure of these attempts; and yet to acknowledge the kernel of truth that lies hid in both—in the authority of the Bible as the record of a gradual self-revelation of God to men, and in the authority of the Church as the living embodiment, spite of all its failures and mistakes, of the work of the Divine Spirit in human hearts. We noted that an Authority present in the life of a living community to-day, is a truer and more satisfying conception than that of an Authority, such as many Protestants have offered us, prisoned in the pages of a Book that comes

Summary

down to us from the past alone. We were constrained to dwell upon the impossible nature of the Protestant appeal to the text of Scripture as final and absolute, and upon the lapse of logic involved in taking as infallible a list of books which is received on the word of the very Church whose authority the Protestant denies. We noted the freedom from this fallacy of the first Reformers, and the liberty with which Luther used the "Testimony of the Spirit" within him to criticise the canon of Scripture which had come to him through the Church of Rome; and we showed how necessary it is that, if the authority of the Bible is to take its right place in our minds, historical criticism should do its work unfettered. It is largely through the light that such study throws upon the sacred writings that the "Testimony of the Spirit" works; because their true meaning, for the most part, can only thus be ascertained. There is indeed enough, and more than enough, in the Bible to help the most unlettered person into living communion with God; but it is only by the aid of historical study, as well as moral insight, that true doctrine can be distinguished; that the clear sunshine of Divine revelation, which is in the Bible, can be separated from the "broken lights," and the distortions of the human media, through which it has come to us.

The refuge which many have thought they had found in the Authority of Christ—that is, in His spoken words when here on earth—we found a vain one. For, even accepting, as we did, that in Jesus

Authority and the Light Within

was incarnated the Eternal Word of God, we yet do not know infallibly what He did say when in the flesh, while we do know that He could only teach such truth as could find lodgment in the imperfect minds of His hearers; and, further, we know that He Himself was compassed with limitations. The attempt to use His recorded words to set at naught the proved results of scientific study, we described as madness. We noted that His first followers made no attempt to erect His words into an infallible oracle, being themselves possessed by His living Spirit, which they trusted as their all-sufficient Guide and Teacher; but that they never supposed this Divine Guide had rendered them infallible, or would teach them without their use of common-sense and the opening of their minds to facts.

Having thus examined the various attempts to establish an infallible outward standard of Authority, we essayed the more difficult task of setting forth, in modern language, what it is that is meant by the Light Within. The words express, as we saw, the human faculty by which knowledge comes to us of objects of thought that are beyond the range of sensuous observation; knowledge of personal character, of general moral duties, of individual "guidance" in particulars, and lastly of God Himself and of life in relation to Him. We described the attempts made by the early Quakers to formulate their discovery of the Light as immediate and personal revelation, and showed how all spiritual teachers are coming more

Summary

and more to recognise that it is in this immediate conscious experience, and not in creeds or opinions, or inferences won by argument, that the knowledge of God consists. The essential truth of Quakerism we found to lie in its recognition that there is something of the Infinite, something of God, in every person; that religion consists in His expanding life in the surrendered soul, and is therefore infinite in its possibilities; that Christianity can never be expressed by any system of dogmatic formulæ. Yet we were compelled to recognise that the early Quakers never rose above the imperfect philosophy of their day, in which the natural and the spiritual worlds were separated by an impassable barrier, and which compelled them to choose between the alternatives of making the Light wholly human and natural, or else wholly Divine and supernatural. They chose the latter, and found themselves shut up to a position which virtually made the individual infallible, leaving no real place for Authority; and which also gravely injured their work by depreciating as unspiritual the use of the human reason, and minimising the need for religious teaching. That in spite of these defects they should have achieved what they did, is the best testimony to the essential truth which they discovered, but which they were unable adequately to express.

We then attempted to find a sound basis for the Light Within in the Idealist philosophy, which, starting from the fact that we have experience of an ordered world, shows that this is only intelligible if what lies beneath it is Mind or Thought—a Universal

Authority and the Light Within

Consciousness, of which each individual consciousness is but an imperfect manifestation. Idealism, therefore, is essentially a doctrine of Divine Immanence; it necessarily posits a Universal Consciousness, which many idealists have no hesitation in calling God, as that without which neither nature nor man would have any real existence. But, while philosophy seems to lay a firm foundation for belief in Immanence, there are some parts of "Divine truth" which appear, as yet, to be beyond its reach; it gives no satisfying account of those disturbing elements in human life which we call Sin and Error; nor has it succeeded in justifying, by cogent reasoning, the certainty which religious experience gives us of the Divine Transcendence. Thus, while Reason in the larger sense of Self-Consciousness is identical with the Inner Light, being both human and divine, there is a more limited sense of the word Reason (that, namely, in which it means *reasoning*) in which they are rightly distinguished; the Inner Light giving us, as it were by intuition or instinctive reason, truths that the slower logical faculty cannot yet cogently demonstrate.

The Light Within, on its human side, may thus be identified with the faculty whose working we call *Faith*, which is "the assurance of things not seen." And it is the part of Faith, not to rule out Reason (in the sense of reasoning) on spiritual matters, but rather to absorb and enlighten it, that it may more effectually do its work of separating the husk from the kernel, and building up a sound theology.

Summary

We then passed to the discussion of some of the difficulties commonly felt in regard to the Light Within: its supposed identity with the Conscience, which gives no fixed and unvarying answer to the questions put to it; its relations to the work wrought out for men by Jesus Christ in the flesh, and to that of His living Spirit in their hearts.

As regards Conscience, we followed the lead of Martineau in distinguishing two meanings of that term, according as it is used for moral perception in general, with a sense of higher and lower in conduct, and the consciousness that we "ought" to pursue the one and avoid the other; or again as the recognition that some particular class of conduct *is* in fact the higher or lower. It was only in the first sense that Conscience could be identified with the Light Within, and even here it covers less ground. In the second or empirical sense, Conscience is the product of environment and education; and, as moral ideas develop, it is continually expanding. The root cause of that development we found in the Light Within, which is ever behind the empirical conscience, leading prophetic souls to embrace ideals higher than those of the conventional morality of their day, and constraining others, not so gifted, to acknowledge the truth of these ideals when presented to them.

The difficulty of relating the Light Within, as the presence of God in every man, with the historic work of Christ on earth which we know as Reconciliation or Atonement, we met by the help of the Johannine conception of the Logos as the Divine Word, which

Authority and the Light Within

has always been with men, through which men in all ages have come to God, and which in the fulness of time became manifested in a perfect human life. It is as we are reconciled to God by Jesus Christ, and as He takes possession of us, that our eyes are opened to see clearly that of which before we were but dimly conscious; it is those whose natures are renewed by the Spirit of the Crucified who come into full possession of their powers of spiritual vision.

Such considerations seem to meet the objection that if all men have the Spirit of God there is no need to try to win them to Jesus Christ. The Light Within is the "earnest" of more to follow; the immanent life of God in man is the "Divine seed" which reaches its flower and fruitage only in the sunshine of conscious Christian experience. This experience brings with it a renewal of the personality; in union with Christ man finds his true self, which *is* in very truth the Holy Spirit abiding in Him. "I live; yet not I, but Christ liveth in me."

In a final chapter we hope to indicate some of the practical bearings of the questions we have been discussing.

XVI

CONCLUSION

WHAT, after all, is the net upshot, and what are the practical bearings, of our long discussion? The questions that have been before us are alive and pressing. We have been endeavouring to find a safe anchorage, "within the veil," for souls that are storm-tossed and drifting, unable to accept the outward authorities that are offered them, but not yet strong enough to trust the Authority within. The number of these drifting souls is increasing fast. The light of scientific criticism is upon the creeds and standards of the past, and they are shrivelling before our eyes. Even in the Roman Church there is a revolt against despotic authority, and a reaching forth after a more inward and spiritual support. In the Protestant churches the number is continually growing of those who know that the Bible is not infallible; but the teachers are few who follow up the lead of the first reformers and can fearlessly point the seekers to the Inward Light.

What we desire is, however feebly it may be done, to help both the seekers, and those (surely they are seekers also) whose duty it is to teach, to a clearer sight of Christianity as essentially the Religion of the Spirit. It is our most earnest desire, in everything that is written, to say nothing that should

Authority and the Light Within

weaken the hold upon any heart of the revelation of God that has come to men through the Christ of history. He remains for us the centre of our faith, the ground of our assurance that we really know the character of God. He satisfies our deepest longings as philosophy can never do, by giving us, at the back of all our problems, not merely a Universal Consciousness but a human heart of love. We recognise His Authority as that of the eternal Word of God. Yet, when we ask how that authority is available for men, we are driven to answer, not through any infallible record of His spoken words when here on earth, but through the presence of His living Spirit in their hearts. It was this essentially that distinguished the religion of His first followers. Apart from His actual life and death, as that of a real human personality in whom (as in no other) God was present, they themselves are wholly unintelligible and unaccounted for; yet it was not in any mechanical reference to the facts or words of that marvellous life that they grounded their authority or found agreement one with another. When any practical problem confronted them, such as the inclusion of Gentile believers and the application to them of the Law of Moses, they never asked "What did the Lord say in the flesh?" but "What does the Spirit say now?" And, in following the Spirit's guidance, they were brought, speaking broadly, into agreement one with another. None of them was rendered infallible; disputes, as between Paul and Peter, were not unknown; but these limitations never upset their serene confidence in the

Conclusion

Inward Guide and Teacher whom their Master had promised them, and whose inspiring presence was a felt reality in their hearts.

The Religion of the Spirit disappeared, and gave place to the Church of the Creeds and of the Middle Ages. A spiritual despotism for centuries held the souls of men in fetters, till the bonds were burst in the mighty outbreak of the Reformation, and man stood erect once more, unshackled, in the presence of his God. For a time it seemed as though, in the exaltation of that new consciousness, the freedom of the early Church was to be recovered. But alas! men were not yet ready for it; and once more their spirits were fettered by the theory of an infallible Book. The uprising of scientific criticism has destroyed that theory for ever, and with it the last possibility of a final outward Authority to regulate men's thoughts and deeds.

What is to be the issue? Surely it can only be in a fearless and trustful return to the position of the first followers of the Master. For this return, the way is open now as it never was before. Whatever criticism has taken from us, it has given us back the personality of Jesus, and an understanding of His consciousness of God, as no century since the first has known it. Whatever have been the mistakes of criticism, it must be recognised as a part of the working of that Spirit which is preparing the souls of men for a larger life, a nobler freedom, and a profounder unity than Christendom has ever known. Let us not plead that we are still unready; let us not

Authority and the Light Within

timorously turn our backs upon the grace and the liberty that God is offering. Let us abandon, once for all, the search for an infallible text-book of truth and duty, and trust ourselves to His Spirit.

Surely this does not mean that we are to throw aside all Authority, and abandon ourselves to an anarchy in which each individual will think and act as he likes. If we make it our first endeavour to come into the place of true discipleship, and to learn, as the first Christians learned, by self-surrender and trust, to share the yoke of Christ and to know that every thought is brought into captivity to His obedience, we shall find, not only rest to our own souls, but fellowship and harmony with our brethren. It is in this conscious Christian experience that we shall enter into a larger life than our own, and find that all we need of Authority comes back to us, in the unity of the Christian consciousness, all down the ages. The Authority of the Bible will be to us no theory reached by painful and sophistical argument, but a living reality felt and accepted, because we have come for ourselves into the experience of which psalmists, prophets and apostles wrote, and understand by spiritual sympathy the truths they struggled to express. The Authority of the Church will be ever round about us, in the collective experience and testimony of all saintly souls who have lived and wrought in the same consciousness of Sonship and in dependence on the same Spirit. Any imagined revelation of our own we shall always be prepared and anxious to test and temper, by comparing it with what

Conclusion

has been revealed to others richer, stronger and more devoted than ourselves, both in the past and present. But to neither Authority shall we ever think of attributing infallibility.

Most of all we shall bow with unmeasured reverence before the Authority of Christ, who has reconciled us to God and brought us into the communion in which Authority regains its meaning. Welcoming all the light which the most careful study can throw upon His person, His work, and His words, we shall shun as irreverence and "pride of heart" the attempt to impose upon history an interpretation due either to the human dogmas that have come to us by tradition, or to negations begotten by a too-limited philosophy of our own. We shall be, at all costs, loyal to the facts we find. Yet this humility and loyalty to truth, though it may lead us to deny some things, and suspend judgment upon others, that have been taught us as true concerning His life on earth, will make us bow in measureless reverence before the person of our Lord and Redeemer, in whom, as in no other,

> We know the fatherhood
> And heart of God revealed.

It is true that, for many of us, our very familiarity with the Gospel pages has robbed them of their freshness, and it is difficult for us to find in them the inspiration, the profound spiritual genius, that is really there. One of the chief services that criticism is rendering is to bring that freshness back, to enable us to drop the scales of familiar tradition, and read

Authority and the Light Within

the gospels with open eyes. Thanks to its aid, many are finding in some of the simplest Gospel stories, so simple as to be intelligible to the youngest child, depths beyond depths of spiritual meaning, and the profoundest knowledge of the human soul and of its most hidden needs. We are constrained to acknowledge that "Never man so spake." One who knows as Jesus knew, who sees with this profundity of spiritual insight, must, we feel, be worthy of our trust. And so to Him belongs without measure that Authority which we concede, in some degree, to all who can see further, and who know more, than others.

And yet this is no blind trust. We do not attain it as, in would-be but mistaken reverence, we close the eyes of our own reason and judgment, and adopt the "credo quia impossibile." It is only ours as in freedom and boldness we use the Light that is given us, and enter into the place of experience and insight where we can see these things in some measure for ourselves, and know that they are not true because Jesus said them, but that He said them because they are true. Deep below all Authority is the Light Within, as that which alone makes it living and not dead, and gives it vital power over our souls. The better we know, by this inner Light, the character of our Master, the more fully shall we understand what it was that inspired His first followers, and the stronger will be our hold upon His present Spirit.

And one yet larger thought remains. Is it not to this purified vision of our Lord that we must look,

Conclusion

and may look with serene confidence, for the true reunion of Christendom? Not by surrender to formal creeds, nor agreement upon ritual observances, shall we know the fulfilment of His prayer, "that they all may be one." Opinions and practices divide, but facts and truth unite. Already, in all Churches, men and women are being drawn together in the fellowship of those who "walk in the Light," who are "of the truth," who have forsaken religions of dogma for the religion of the Spirit. Below all our surface differences there is the substantial unity of those who worship the same Lord, whose minds are open to the same facts, who have been lifted by Him into the same Christian experience, which is fellowship with the Father and with His Son Jesus Christ.

"If we walk in the Light, as He is in the Light, we shall have fellowship one with another," because our spiritual eyes are opened through an inward experience of His "blood," which "cleanseth us from all sin."

INDEX

	PAGE
APOSTLES, seldom quote Jesus	55—57, 122
Atonement, early Quakers on	113, 114
as Reconciliation	114—116
as enlightening	116—119
Authority, its Nature	11—17
true place of	138—141
Autonomy of the Individual	13, 14, 63
Barclay, Robert, and "The Apology"	38
on the Bible	39, 40
on the Light Within	72, 73, 118
Bible, as the "Word of God"	30
infallibility impossible	30—33
and the Quakers	37—42
Calvin and the Bible	28, 33
Church, Roman ideas of	18—25
Anglican ,,	24, 25
Criticism, necessary	41—44
and the Person of Jesus	48, 49
Depravity, doctrine of	99, 112
Dualism of early Quakers	80—83
Faith and Reason	101—103, 132
Fox, George, on the Bible	37
on the Light Within	71, 72
Idealism	89, 90, 96, 97
Immanence of God	75
Infallibility of the Church	18—24
of the Bible	27—34
of the Individual	83, 84
Inspiration in the early Church	59—62, 122
Inward Witness to truth of Bible	29, 33, 35, 40—45
Kenosis of Christ	52
Knowledge of God	15, 16, 67—69, 89—92

Index

	PAGE
Light Within, meaning	63—69
and the Quakers	70—87
and modern religious teachers	74
Logos, doctrine of the	60, 116, 117, 121
Luther and the Bible	28, 29
Old Testament and Christ's Authority	46, 47
Protestant ideas of the Bible	27—30, 35, 36, 45, 46
Quakerism, essence of	76
Quakers on the Bible	37—42
Reason, place of	99—103
Reformers on the Bible	28—30, 33—36
Religion of the Spirit	135—141
Silence of God	58
Sin	93—99
Socrates and the "daimon"	67
Spirit, The, meaning	59—62, 121, 124
in the early Church	60, 61
Transcendence of God	97, 98

CPSIA information can be obtained
at www.ICGtesting.com
Printed in the USA
LVOW04s2310150117
521067LV00033B/1557/P